BOWLFUL OF LAUGHS

A TRAVELER'S TRAUMATIC
TOILET TALES

Bill Rosen and Marie Thomas

BOWLFUL OF LAUGHS

A TRAVELER'S TRAUMATIC
TOILET TALES

Bill Rosen and Marie Thomas

Alycat Publishing
Framingham, MA 01702

COVER AND INSIDE ILLUSTRATIVE CREDITS
Cover design by Marie Thomas, Al Snyder, Leann Webb
Creative artwork by Al Snyder and Leann Webb

Interior design by White Cottage Publishing Company
www.whitecottagepublishing.com
Edited by Marie Thomas

Bowlful of Laughs — A Traveler's Traumatic Toilet Tales /
Bill Rosen and Marie Thomas
ISBN: 978-0-9889778-0-8 hard cover
ISBN: 978-0-9889778-1-5 soft cover

Library of Congress Control Number: 2013937881
1. Toilet 2. Traveler's Tales 3. Humor 4. Laughs 5. Adults 6. Children

Alycat Publishing
Humor Division
Framingham, Massachusetts 01702
www.alycatpublishing.org

Multiple copy discounts, contact: alycatpub@verizon.net

Printed in the United States for Worldwide Distribution

Dedication

To my very best friend, Howard Bernstein,
who always encouraged me and stuck by me through
thick and thin. I can never thank you enough.

— *Bill Rosen*

Acknowledgments

My co-author Marie Thomas and I would like to acknowledge, with gratitude, the members of our talented and creative illustrating team, whose wit and artistic ingenuity meshed so well and enjoyably with our own to turn out this book: artist-supreme Al Snyder, and illustrator-extraordinaire, "WebbWoman", the inimitable Leann Webb. [webbwoman61@yahoo.com]

I would also like to thank Neil Lerner, an accomplished photographer and my longtime friend, who always told me to get into writing. Your encouragement clicked one day and I'm grateful.

My special thanks also, to my insightful creative writing teacher, Domenic Corsaro, whose own talent and enthusiasm was contagious to me and who single-handedly inspired me "to be a writer." Along with my parents' encouragement, Domenic's proved invaluable and has herein finally born published fruit. Coincidentally, Domenic himself has just published his first novel[1] as well.

---

[1] *The Bible According to Nick Santangelo*, by Domenic Corsaro, published December 2012.

Thank you especially to my longtime friend, Rachel Simon[2], writer, for your warm encouragement and consistent enthusiasm whenever we discussed my writing endeavors. You put the fuel in my tank for me to pursue writing as an achievable reality.

We also gratefully acknowledge the insightful comments and review by Edward R. Rogaishio, prolific fine artist, author, poet, and inscrutable humorist.

And our thanks to Jo Reaves, who tirelessly put all this together for us for printing. An amazing job!

Last, but not least, my dearest Raelene from Vancouver. The best cousin ever! You have more than my thanks; your love, kindness, friendship, and encouragement have been irreplaceable.

---

[2]Award-winning author of two bestsellers, *Riding the Bus With My Sister*, August, 2003, and *The Story of Beautiful Girl*, February, 2012.

Preface

As a preschooler I was a free man. Life was a never-ending dream. I was an adventurer, an explorer searching for the fountain of old age. Each floor was a universe, every room a world with furniture, machines, new tastes, smells, treasures, and dangers, some hidden, some gloriously exposed.

Mark Twain said "I have never let my schooling interfere with my education" and I knew this intrinsically since I learned to walk. I just couldn't tell anyone because I hadn't learned to talk yet. But this made little difference as I waddled along on my daily quest in that big old house on Benson Street in Camden, New Jersey.

Of all my discoveries, I dove headlong into what I now know of as "major appliances." Every floor had them although they seemed to congregate on the lower floors. Each had a specific purpose. Some of these machines produced warm air, others provided cold air, some washed the dishes, and one even opened cat food cans.

A couple of appliances were off-limits and I was forbidden to investigate them so I had to wait until my Mom was talking on that thing that looked like a shoe (and had a curly wire anchoring it to the main unit). I'd just raise my eyebrows, shove my hands in my pockets, whistle a tune, and slowly enter the center of the universe: the bathroom. This is where the toilet lived.

One look at this massive white porcelain contraption and I knew we'd put a man on the moon one day. I began flushing small things down the toilet; tissues, paper cups, toy dinosaurs, but large strong arms quickly sabotaged my efforts to drown my pajamas. The toilet threw up and I got sent to my room.

Aside from traveling abroad, I have crossed the length and breadth of this nation several times and am uniquely qualified to elaborate on this subject. In the decades that followed, as if in retribution, I was hounded, pursued, and assaulted by toilets from coast to coast, at work and in the home. I later came to know toilets on a personal level in eight states from Canada to the Rio Grande. If only I'd had a user's manual for toilets. Not once did I find an instruction manual or troubleshooting chart when things decided to go wrong; hence, the reason for writing this book. As a patriotic American, I felt it was my civic duty to provide this information.

I compiled these enlightening adventures from real-life, both humorous and realistic, to enlighten the reader on how to handle similar situations and any unsettling repercussions that might ensue. Thus this becomes a fun-filled textbook whose rightful berth is on the back of every toilet in the New World. If "into every life some rain must fall," this book is your umbrella.

Here are eighteen entertaining and comprehensive 'toilet encounters of the 4th kind', along with colorful illustrations. Each one is the appropriate reading length to empty a healthy digestive tract. In this way the average reader (or parent) can find the help they are looking for between its covers.

— *Bill Rosen*

Table of Contents

The Potty Parade

~~~~~~~~~~~

"A natural born comedian like his dad", people said about my son. I like to think the acorn didn't fall far from the tree, and I had good reason to believe my son was destined to make people laugh—maybe someday take to the stage to bring humor into the lives of many. He was funny even when he wasn't trying to be.

He was barely two and still needed a booster chair at home (or a phone book when visiting) to help him reach his plate at the table. And even at such a young age, as soon as he could talk, he could tell jokes. (And what a crowd pleaser!) The audience would faithfully drip with smiles, and politely applaud right after he delivered his punch line with pin-point timing. When most kids were trying to get the right shoe on the right foot, he was already 'working the audience.'

Once, when his mom and I took him fishing with us in a small boat, we were stunned by what came out of his mouth. Far from our vacation cabin and just moments after we dropped anchor, my wife made the grisly discovery we had forgotten to bring refreshments for our little blonde tyke. We had brought coffee for ourselves, but in the rush, my wife and I had each assumed the other had packed his beverage of choice - apple juice.

1

Still in diapers and wrestling with how to pronounce people's names, our little angel watched us with interest as we explored our options and came to the bitter realization that all we had on board was full-strength coffee. No parent in their right mind would ever give coffee to a kid who didn't know kindergarten from kangaroo. We looked at the thermos, we looked at my son, we looked at each other. As we tried to figure this one out, his polite little voice piped up and said "I'd prefer decaffeinated." We practically fell out of the boat!

And he didn't stop here. Several years later we received a phone call one evening after dinner. A friend of mine called and my son got to answer the phone. This often confused the caller at first, but we knew it was a real thrill to someone who's still learning to tie his shoes. Once we knew it was my friend calling and greetings were out of the way, my friend asked our little telephone host, who was then in Kindergarten and learning his ABC's, "So what are you up to?" My son's honest reply came back instantly "S's."

Another time, when picking him up at a friend's house after school, I began collecting his belongings as he sat on the floor pulling on his sneakers. I got distracted talking to another adult and failed to realize he'd gotten his sneakers reversed. When I finally realized what had happened and told him that his sneakers were on the wrong feet, he shot back "They're the only ones I have."

He wasn't alone either—it seemed the rest of my kids also had talent. His older sister in the fifth grade often went food shopping with me. She was a rare pleasure to take along. While I was shopping, I'd send her off on missions (we called them 'assignments') that would take her back to aisles where we had been. On one such outing, she suddenly sprang a big shocker on me and informed me that she wanted to "go to Karate."

Now this is a big decision, and especially without her mother there, it was nothing to be answered lightly. I began by trying to do my best to convey to her everything I knew about the Martial Arts (which wasn't a lot). A little more than halfway through my speech, she held up her hand as if to say "stop" and said "I meant Hawaii, Hawaii, not Karate."

And the fun didn't stop with my own kids. During some "backyard banter" as I compared notes with my neighbors, it was like an episode of Hee Haw as we discovered all our kids had the same propensities. Some of the greatest stories I've ever heard often came as a direct result of just going out to cut the grass. It was amazing how we would start out here and wind up there.

When I'd begin chatting with a neighbor on a serious subject like the kids' school, we'd soon digress to tales of digestive woe, and end up discussing the potty parade. It was probably like this since cave man days. Suitably, toward the end of such conversations, each party would take turns trying to outdo the other with their children's tales, anything that provoked disgust, horror, laughter, or blood. It was like group therapy in a way: a cathartic release–the sort of thing that kids do on a continual basis and manage to stay on track, but it's good for parents too. It's true, we can learn from our children.

Bowlful of Laughs

While my stories could claim first place for toilets getting clogged, my neighbor's son was way out ahead with his personal clogging problems. On one occasion, my neighbor was relating the difficult obstacles his son had overcome back in the potty training days. Apparently he was prone to consuming large amounts of peanut butter, which was thought to be the culprit here, even though none of us really had a clue.

Our clogged toilets were the result of the toilets being fed all the kids' toys from building-blocks, toy cars, G.I. Joe dolls, and various sizes of plastic dinosaurs, while my neighbor's kid's plumbing was fighting more edible demons. Although cured easily enough, constipation is nothing to laugh at, and in the early stages can evolve into fear, even horror, to an innocent inductee.

As the story went, his son was in the bathroom for an unusually long time and questions were being raised. Parents have eyes in the back of their heads and when you hear the bathroom door slam, your ears automatically begin a discussion with these eyes. Respecting the child's privacy is important, so his mom hesitated before lightly knocking and carefully listening to the performance through the door. She heard an exceptional amount of grunting and panting and it was instantly clear the boy was straining with everything he had to get the job done.

His mom rapped on the door and politely inquired 'Everything okay in there?', although she was fairly certain what scenario was being played out: tight little fists, little red face all out of breath, scrunched up eyebrows and tightly closed eyes... Silence from the other side. "Are you having a hard time in there?" she asked. A moment later a small, but clearly scared, voice replied "Yeah, I think I'm having a hard-attack!" Zing!

My neighbor barely had time to take a breath before I quickly came back with a little story about a long drive from Philly to Brattleboro, Vermont in a full-sized Detroit mega-monster station wagon packed with a group of 7-year-olds that rivaled the entire second grade in terms of numbers. This was before we had the sense to use seat belts, and it was common practice to pack kids into cars like sardines. It was an age of innocence and ignorance all in one.

We were driving north on New Jersey's Garden State Parkway that wound left and right, up and down, all around town, and came to abrupt stops at what seemed like every twenty feet to throw thirty-five cents into the toll collection basket before hitting the gas and accelerating again. Soon this jolting roller-coaster ride began taking its toll and the kids' stomachs began rumbling. Then somewhere between East Orange and West Orange, all hell broke loose.

One of the kids in the rear-facing rumble seat tossed his cookies and immediately the titanic cruiser was filled with the familiar stench of parmesan cheese. Moans, groans, and even hysterical laughter rippled through the crowd. I was driving so my hands were tied. All I could do was help-lessly look for a rest stop while another adult tried to calm the bedlam—but to little avail amidst the wails of laughter and disgust. This was when I learned of the Domino Effect on a car full of children. Within the next few minutes the smell had nauseated all the others and soon we got to see what nearly everybody'd had for lunch.

Not to be outdone, my neighbor came back with his "classic tale" that I had heard before (but didn't mind hearing again). It took place around the time his young son just got brave enough to say "bye-bye" to his plastic potty ensemble and, with his parents' help, he climbed up on the adult version – a gleaming ceramic monument to man's ingenuity. He made the transition just as things began binding up inside, maybe partially due to stage fright.

It's true many small children fear the very size of the standard toilet, so much more grandiose than their familiar little plastic seat that just fits their tiny hiney. Maybe the fear of slipping and falling backward into the abyss sparked more than a measure of caution and simply put a halt to the countdown. For whatever the reason, the little kid kept smacking his forehead every twenty seconds or so with the palm of his hand. Concerned, his dad asked why he kept hitting his head. His son looked up and replied "It works for the bottle of ketchup." Moments later he was victorious.

That was a great story and it wouldn't be easy to top, so I had to tap into my own plastic potty experience when I was making my transition from diapers. I can still remember how my mom was nice enough to patiently introduce me to the new contraption. She walked me through the entire process and then answered my questions. And she even put the potty in my bedroom 'so', she said, 'all I had to do was hop out of bed, lower my jammy pants and sit'. She seemed so proud of me that I was now big enough to

not have to wake her up to get potty help in the middle of the night, that I hated to tell her. The only problem for me was that at night I faced my greatest fear – lobster attacks from under my bed.

7

It was clear that to take advantage of this new convenience, I still had to clean up by myself and go wash my hands. But that was only if I was fairly certain there weren't any rogue lobsters around – and I never was. So in spite of my graduation, this still meant getting my mom. Children bond to their mothers naturally, but this was a time in my life that I was locked onto her - I was in awe of her unbridled protectiveness for me in the face of such a deadly threat.

She knew the drill by heart. With a broom and a flashlight, she would come bravely into my room and get down on the floor, swinging that broom under the bed and yelling "Lobsters, get out!" I'd stay a few feet behind her, knowing a lobster would have to get past my heroic mom before reaching me. At that age, I had never witnessed such unbelievable bravery in the face of a lobster. I felt completely safe. She made sure the night light was close to the potty so I wouldn't have any problems, and left after the usual tuck-in and kiss.

But by 3 a.m., the worst happened again. There I was, suddenly wide awake and requiring the use of the facilities. I had to be a man. I got on my belly and swung my feet over the side of the bed, pointing my toes to reach the floor. I prepared myself and carefully sat down on the cold little potty seat. Slowly looking around, I realized I had company. There was a gigantic shadow on the wall to my left. It looked like a giant man on a giant toilet. I hesitantly waved my hand and the giant waved his hand back. I stood up, and the giant stood up. Then, no time for games, we both sat down again and got down to business—I knew my mom would take care of mine, but I couldn't help wondering who would clean up what the giant had left behind.

No—Not That Button!

~~~~~~~~~~~

My parents had recently divorced and were going through that stage where each did their honest best to outdo the other in terms of my entertainment. I realized that this form of confirming their love to me was really necessary to satisfy something inside each of them. Fortunately, I was already tuned into it.

I guess it is part of the "growing up" that parents have to do. I enjoyed the ride while it lasted; appreciative, and applauding their efforts whether extravagant or meager. I was easy—so I went with the flow. Burgers or night flights were equally acceptable, and even at the fresh age of nine I understood it was the thought that counts. I knew the difference between bananas and bonanza. This was clearly a bonanza that I had never dared to dream of.

My dad clearly won out temporarily when he told me about his plans to take me to Key West and go fishing in December. I nearly passed out. To a fourth grader from Philly, a week's trip to Florida during the holidays to go fishing with my dad was the best deal to come down the pike in my whole life. Not only would I miss an additional day or two of school, and go fishing, but it would be just my dad and me. I could actually hear my heart pounding. And I could barely believe my ears when I learned we were going to "fly", as my dad put it so nonchalantly.

To a nine-year-old there's absolutely nothing as thrilling as your first ride in an airplane. This was the big-time—the real thing. You've graduated from "Are we there yet?" to "How fast are we going?" and "How high up are we?" You eat life or life eats you, and this was nothing less than the loin of adventure—the very threshold to manhood. The roller coaster and the Ferris wheel were toys; but snapping the seat belt closed on a Lockheed L-188 Electra Turbo Prop in a seat by the window was the real McCoy, and not for the faint of heart.

We would fly non-stop from Philadelphia International to Miami International, at night no less. How much more exciting could it be? Next we'd rent a car, stay in a hotel overnight, and then drive to Ilslamorada, midway between Miami and Key West. Bathing suit weather in December! Sometime during the week he said, we'd drive the additional seventy-five miles to Key West and go sightseeing. My dad had worked out all the logistics, right down to renting fishing rods, the kind of fish we'd catch, and what type of car we'd drive. I was the luckiest kid in the world—the envy of the block. And no homework!

Even though it must have hurt my mom in a way only parents are vulnerable to, she okayed the adventure and helped me make a list of all the unimportant things I'd never have thought of myself, like clothes, toothbrush, soap, and shampoo. Even at my age, I was mature enough to see the necessity of my penknife, flashlight, some comic books, a canteen, my camera, and my lucky penny. But I politely allowed my mom to contribute and smiled to myself at her earnest packing efforts and good intentions for my well being, no matter how ridiculous. I even looked the other way when she insisted I take along some dress clothes. I mean, honestly! Do swordfish really care what you're wearing while you reel them in?

It was a hundred and fifty miles from Miami to Key West, a string of islands all connected by one road, the famous Route 1. Ilslamorada was a good three hour drive south with the Atlantic Ocean on the left and the Gulf of Mexico on the right. Somewhere in the package was the famous Seven Mile Bridge.

As vacation time grew closer, my mind began to drift off and at school I was frequently caught staring into space. I missed the entire Geography chapter on Nebraska, Kansas, and Iowa. Social Studies just lost its "zing", and while the rest of the class was discussing beef, hogs, corn, and the Platte River, I was hauling in Sergeant Majors and Groupers, and climbing palm trees. When they got to the spine-tingling part about Kansas oil fields, prairie fires, and Longhorn cattle, I was keeping my line taught as a hundred-pound Sailfish flew eight feet out of the water and sparkled in the bright Florida sun.

I vaguely recalled something about Iowa leading the country in chickens, popcorn, and something to do with breakfast cereal, but I was struggling to hold up a Marlin bigger than I was while my beaming dad took pictures (several, in case the first one didn't come out). By the third or fourth time the teacher called my name, I was yanked rudely back to reality and didn't have a clue as to what part of the country we were in. This was around the time I learned that passing notes in class was against the law, but my teacher flagrantly disregarded this law and gave me one to hand deliver to my mom at home. It wasn't a love note or a drawing of an elephant either.

In a surprise Geography quiz a day later, I totally blew it when I wrote about Robert E. Peary hacking his way through the jungle in search of the North Pole. My teacher didn't buy it and I was forced at gunpoint to re-read an entire chapter and write a full-page report about the 1909 expedition. I think she caught onto me because everyone knows that the jungle was at the South Pole.

By departure day, Saturday, December 23rd, my head was in the clouds all the time—thinking about the ride in the airplane. At some point the plane began to "take flight" in my mind and managed to eclipse everything else we had planned. Soon the ride in the plane began taking on more meaning than the fishing or the entire vacation week in Florida; the flight itself became the adventure and commandeered all other dreams and fantasies my mind invented.

In my mind's eye I saw the pilot becoming ill and I was called into the cockpit to take command of the plane, seeming to understand all the instruments, skillfully causing it to dip and soar by sheer guts and instinct, performing this daunting task that I had never done before. Even at nine I knew the steering wheel wasn't round like the ones in a car, and if you pushed it in toward the dashboard the plane went down, and if you pulled it back toward you the plane would head upward or gain altitude. I supposed if you turned it left the whole thing would go left. How much more complicated could it be? I don't think they had turn signals or windshield wipers to contend with.

I had learned quite a bit from watching television and going to the movies. John Wayne could ride a horse, drive a car, fly a plane, and shoot a gun all at the same time. I fully respected my dad's intentions and didn't dare let on that I was actually more excited about our flight than anything else. As far as I was concerned, once we got there we'd kill a week until it was time to board another plane for the thrilling ride home.

When the day of departure finally arrived I was more nervous than excited. I also had a stiff neck from watching planes and everything else up in the wild blue yonder all the previous weeks. Then excitement gave way to apprehension once I learned we would not each have our own parachute. I knew that could easily become a life and death situation. After all, cars broke down without warning, might this also be a possibility up there in the sky? Planes might have engine problems like cars, and I knew what a busted fan belt and an overheated radiator looked like.

When we arrived, it was clear that Philadelphia International Airport was a big place, probably larger than my entire elementary school. On my best behavior, I walked a straight line and stayed close by my dad, anxious to obey, eager to learn. Planes roared as they took off and roared as they landed and everyone there felt the excitement in the air. My heart raced, the adrenalin pumped, and my voice cracked. There was no turning back now, and I fully realized, if push came to shove, I doubted I actually could fly one of these babies. Thank God for co-pilots.

By now our luggage was checked in and my dad was amazingly calm. A world traveler, he had flown many times and even cracked some jokes to keep me calm. I laughed mechanically once I detected the punch line had been delivered. The magazine my dad bought me was soon slippery with sweat. I grabbed for it several times as my tight little fist kept losing its grip, and stared out the window at the bustle on the tarmac, thinking these might be my final moments before meeting God face to face. My dad sensed my nervousness and got me a candy bar, which I ate distractedly as I dreaded what was ahead and wished we had already arrived at our destination.

Like a condemned man, I dutifully followed my dad after we showed our tickets at the gate. I checked to make sure he was behind me as we approached the telescoped boarding chute to the plane. If he chickened out at the last moment, I didn't intend to get on board by myself. I felt a little dizzy, but placed one foot in front of the other following the lady in front of me.

Just as I was about to step off the declining walkway, I glanced down at the gap between the gangplank and the plane and saw an abyss that looked like it went a hundred feet down. If I hadn't felt my dad's reassuring hand on my elbow I might have bolted, but there was no turning back. My life was no longer in my own hands. Man and machine controlled my destiny. I tried to gulp, but my mouth was dry.

We got to our row and I took the seat by the window on the port side of the plane. I knew it was the port side because my dad had told me both "port" and "left" contain four letters, but the word itself meant nothing. I groped for the seat belt and snapped it closed around me while there were still passengers waiting in line to board. I wasn't taking any chances.

After a long wait while everyone got settled, suddenly we heard the engines revving and the plane began its taxi to the runway. The revving got louder and the plane's speed increased and I began to enjoy the feeling of its surging motion. The take-off was exhilarating and unmatched to anything I had ever experienced, although some of my mom's maneuvers in our `54 Ford Crestliner were pretty breathtaking on occasion.

We rose at a steep incline that made me gasp and I found myself leaning forward to catch glimpses of the ground and the buildings that I wouldn't see again until we returned in a week. After we climbed through some thin clouds, the sky cleared and we leveled out flying over the Atlantic. The bright sparkling water went on and on, but after a while the expansive view became a little monotonous. As it got later and darker, it was even a little disappointing to see nothing but reflections of myself in the tiny window.

For the next two hours to Miami, there was just that familiar looking nine-year-old boy looking back at me and mimicking my every movement. Frankly, when it became anti-climactic, I realized I had to pee badly. I had been so intent on this new experience, I had been holding it in for quite some time. Nature wasn't just calling, suddenly it was shouting.

I squeezed past my dad and the man next to him and tried to carefully keep my balance as I walked toward the rear of the plane where the restroom was. The stewardess (now they call them flight attendants) kindly opened the door for me and I went inside. I was amazed at how I accidentally wound up in the kids' restroom where things seemed to be a more comfortably normal size than the usual restrooms designed for giants. Everything was laid out perfectly and I didn't have to walk anywhere, just turn from where I had stood to relieve myself and wash my hands.

Then I saw it. Directly above the toilet was an important-looking button—no label, just a menacing button on a wall inside an airplane, that happened to be located in the restroom. Common sense said it had to do with flushing the toilet, but common sense also said "if you don't know what this button does, don't press it!" In an instant I was sweating.

The plane was jostling around a little more than before so I held my breath, closed my eyes, and reached for the button. At the exact instant my finger touched the button, it felt like we'd hit a big speed bump and I was sure I had unwittingly caused the plane to swerve off the road. For an entire five seconds I stood there clinging to the sink, frozen with fear, thinking it was curtains for everyone. And it was all my fault for pressing the "crash button."

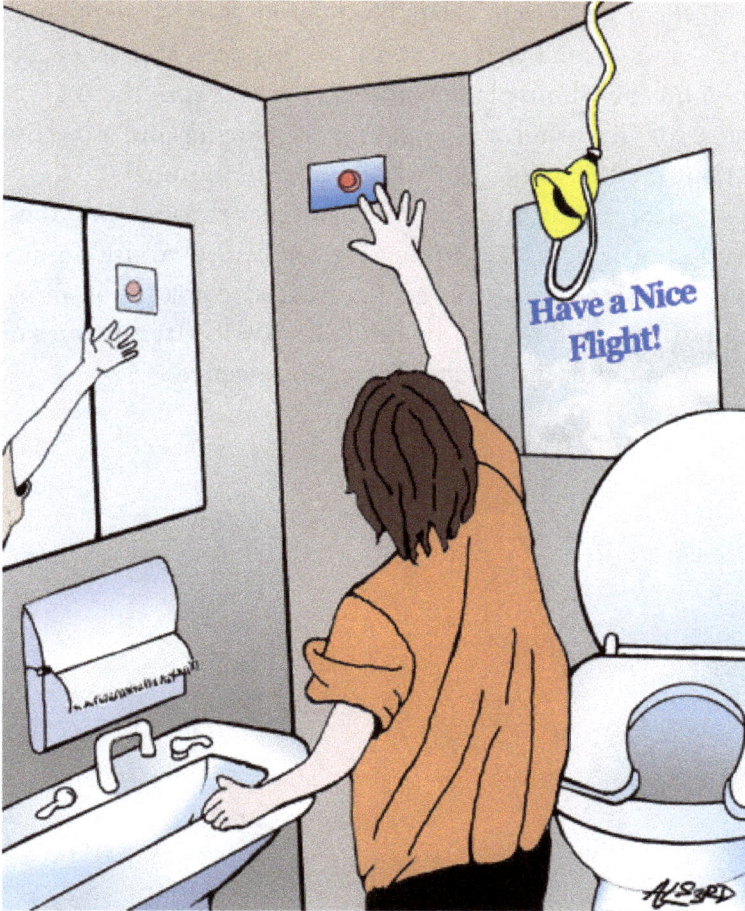

When the bumping and thumping calmed down and I got up the courage to exit and return to my seat, I found out about "air pockets" and how they affect airplanes—but not before I had confessed my actions and fears to my very composed dad and learned how my ignorance of air travel affected him.

First he just chuckled, but then he started laughing so hard and so loud that tears came to his eyes. Worse, everyone on the whole plane could hear him. From there I was sure all the other passengers were staring and tittering about me the whole way to Miami International.

Scarred for life, this scenario races through my mind and almost paralyzes me whenever I need to use an airplane restroom. But as an adult, it also made me more mindful of, and hopefully more compassionate, at times of my own childrens' 'technological innocence'.

Those Stinkin' Varmints

~~~~~~~~~~~

Spending the summer in Saskatchewan with my cousin Raelene was the highlight of every year when I was in grade school. I grew up in Philadelphia and those excursions into the hinterlands of Canada were the adventures of a lifetime. It brought out the Daniel Boone in me.

Getting there was an adventure of its own, entailing train, bus, a short flight in a small plane, and the final leg in a back-firing old pickup truck that just barely managed to reach its destination, my aunt and uncle's farm.

There was a two-day trip with a stopover in Grand Forks, Minnesota in a rundown motel, but at the ripe old age of ten, that was just one more exciting experience that added to the adventure as we headed for the great wooded North. The old flea-bag motel had water pipes that banged in the walls at night like rowdy railroad gandy dancers.

By the time I was about 14, my parents sent me off alone with a list of instructions and phone numbers and made me swear on my life to call at each stop. But in the beginning they came with me and visited with my aunt and uncle for the day before returning home. Of all the dangers that prevailed in this journey, the hotel turned out to be the greatest threat of all. The last time I went up, at the age of 16, I found just a dirt field where the rickety old place once stood. Rumor had it, somebody slammed a door and the place collapsed. Fortunately, a friendly neighbor family put me up that year.

From Grand Forks, a bush pilot would fly us to Regina. This was without a doubt the most exciting part of the trip. Once the old pilot allowed me to take the yoke and actually steer for a few minutes, so now I felt qualified to pilot a plane.

In Regina, Raelene's Grandpa Fred would be waiting in his ancient Dodge pickup with the missing tailgate. From the air we could see a bale of hay, sacks of grain, some tools, and various unidentifiable but important-looking parts of machinery in the truck bed. I secretly thought Grandpa Fred was a scientist on the brink of great inventions involving gears, cogs, levers and chain.

Two cokes and an hour's drive later as Grandpa Fred brought us up to date with his riveting stories of wolves, coyotes, bears, and raccoons, we arrived at their homestead carved out of the wilderness. Bear and wolf stories always held a special interest for me because I could take home the funny–and not so funny–situations he depicted, to retell to my bulging-eyed friends when I returned to the city at the end of August. I embellished with stories of Big Foot, but saved the 'mysterious lights in the sky' for the grand finale.

A warm welcome always awaited us, and I hugged each member of the clan, my aunt and uncle, (Raelene's mom and dad), Raelene's brother Dennis, and especially Raelene, my favorite cousin and best friend who took me on exciting journeys through the forest to swimming holes, dark spooky mountain caves, wild blueberry bush lands, and raspberry fields. The grownups always said how much older I looked and I'd return the compliment and tell them how much older they looked too.

Raelene took me down to the barn and introduced me to all their new animals and let me feed the chickens, the goat, and the friendly cow. 'Someday', she said, I could even 'ride the horse'. I recall the day this was supposed to happen, and I have a bump on the back of my head as a reminder.

This particular late summer afternoon when I was ten, after Mom and Dad said their goodbyes and Grandpa Fred drove them back to the airfield to head for home, it was getting a little dark. Part of freshening up included a short trip to the outhouse, which although quite a novelty, was not my favorite place. There were inhabitants of the rustic little building that always bothered me.

I had no particular fear of spiders as long as they remained a respectable size, but when they were as big as squirrels like the ones up there, whatever fascination they might have held vanished. They were unbelievably revolting and what they lacked in beauty, they made up for in attitude and they could take off at a really nice clip in any direction at the slightest provocation. They acted as if the outhouse belonged to them and I was the intruder. Once I got up the courage to pay attention to how they were looking at me, I began to agree with them.

I'm sure I blocked out of my mind what they really looked like, but I can remember the characteristics because Rae and I used to sing a song about them to the tune of Partridge In A Pear Tree that went something like:

On the first night of camp, little voices sang to me
"Come to the woods and make peeeee".
And I really couldn't wait so I ha-a-add to go
And I headed for the owow-outhouse.

But the second that I got there, the spiders came to me,
With ugly globby he-eads
Two-inch furry bodies
Three red beady eyes
Four biting clinchers
FIVE POI-SON FANGS!
Sticky, yukky webs
Seven nasty friends
Ei-eight friggin' legs
And they drooled and galloped 'round the outhouse!

It was pretty hard to see inside the small building, and the typical stench was almost overpowering. It was nothing to someone who was used to it, but those first few days were always a challenge.

Those Stinkin' Varmints

After getting seated, I looked around and the dozen or so spiders looked as if they were gathering for an attack. The batteries in the old flashlight flickered ominously the whole time. I had to smack the flashlight every few minutes or risk being stranded in the dark, which scenario I'm sure the spiders anxiously awaited. I finished my business, tore some pages from the Sears catalog, cleaned up, and got out of there.

The travel had worn me out and the early bedtime commonly observed on farms was certainly welcome. A wink from Raelene as Dennis and Rae and I ran upstairs for bed was all that my imagination needed and I knew she had many adventures planned for the weeks ahead. I felt for my pocketknife in my jeans for reassurance and turned in using the upper bunk in Dennis's bedroom. It was a cool breezy night and the covers were warm and heavy. I think I fell asleep instantly.

The next morning, after a good country breakfast of toast and fresh farm eggs, Raelene raced me out to the barn to see the animals, which consumed the entire morning. Their hound dogs didn't see strangers often, so they came along to watch me. The livestock, the loft, the earthy odors of hay and manure, the equipment, the tools, the trap doors and pulleys, the rope.... there was more than enough to keep us hypnotically occupied until her mom rang the lunch bell.

That bell meant you were to drop whatever you were doing and make a beeline for the table. Oddly, as we arrived, Grandpa was heading quite briskly in the opposite direction down the grassy path to the outhouse, a sense of urgency in his stride.

Hands and face washed, Raelene and I sat side by side
at the table, swinging our legs, talking and joking, and rav-
enously inhaling the thick smell of beef brisket on fresh
baked rolls. It was only polite to wait for everyone, so wait
we did. Dennis was off at the fishing hole and Raelene's dad
was at work so Raelene, her mom, and I waited for Grandpa
Fred who seemed to be taking a little longer than usual to
return. When our stomachs began to growl, it wasn't long
before we were whining about the delay. We began sipping
the cold milk by our plates.

Finally, Raelene's mom suggested we go see what was
taking Grandpa so long. "Perhaps he fell in…" she said. Raelene and I took this quite literally and had certainly looked
down in there and knew it was no place anyone in their right
mind would ever want to be trapped. We raced heroically
out the door toward the outhouse to rescue dear Grandpa.

A good twenty feet away, we came to a screeching
halt as the situation became crystal clear. There, outside
the outhouse door was what looked like a 40-pound skunk,
up on its hind legs and clawing at the door trying to get
in. Grandpa's voice seemed a little higher than usual as
he yelled and screamed trying to chase off the skunk with
absolutely no success. The skunk was just as determined as
Grandpa. The skunk wanted in, Grandpa wanted out.

We asked what we could do and were told to "get
back" and "do not call the dogs." Skunked dogs would be
no picnic to deal with. So from a little distance, we watched
the skunk eventually leave the door and come back a few
times, circling the outhouse and then returning. It either
really liked Grandpa or had it in for him.

After watching, we snuck a little closer to yell to him what was happening, and to point out that the skunk seemed to spend more time behind rather than in front of the outhouse, so we said we'd tell him when the skunk was out of sight so he could make a run for it. He immediately found this idea appealing and gave us orders to alert him when the coast was clear.

At the precise moment the skunk disappeared around the back corner, Raelene and I shouted in unison "Grandpa, RUN!" The door burst open, nearly getting ripped off the hinges, and Grandpa Fred fled with one hand holding up his drawers and the other waving in the air shooing us down the trail with an enthusiasm rarely seen in him before. We all ran like our lives depended on it. Had we looked back, we'd have seen the skunk, hardly perturbed, peering quizzically at us from the far edge of the outhouse.

Once inside the safety of the kitchen, Raelene's mom looked anxiously from face to face as we all eagerly talked at once. The moment she realized what had happened she started laughing hysterically and couldn't stop. The more serious we got, the more she laughed, until tears were streaming down her face and she had to wipe them away with her apron.

This only made Grandpa angry and he yelled at her that this could have happened to her, which sobered her up a bit. Skunks were 'not to be trifled with' he said knowingly. Aside from the noxious stream of odor they could disperse, he insisted, they were alarmingly accurate and 'aimed for the eyes'.

Raelene and I exchanged glances and tried our best to stop giggling. The laughing subsided, but nobody had to relieve themself for a long time; at least not until early the next morning when Grandpa, armed with his rifle and his good running shoes, snuck out to the outhouse to investigate.

Those Stinkin' Varmints

Much to his surprise he discovered the skunk actually lived there! She had apparently taken up residence in the outhouse and was nursing a litter of five kits. Grandpa realized that the small pile of debris he noticed in the corner there before he fled may have had her young in it! We later guessed that since skunks are voracious insect eaters, the huge globby-headed spiders may have been her favorite fast food, and I, for one, suddenly found that an admirable characteristic. Why go for take-out when you can live at the restaurant?

But after all our yelling and Grandpa's noisily bursting out the door the way he did, Mrs. Skunk seemed happy to give us all a wide berth and had moved her young out of the 'upstairs' to underneath the back of the building. Since that was where the worst odor was, we all began to feel sorry for her.

But, the skunk family got used to our intermittent presence as her babies grew up in the basement, and then as soon as their little legs could travel, they all quickly moved away. Wouldn't you?

So for about the next six weeks, through careful (extremely careful), use of the outhouse, we found we could all coexist and share the building as needed. It was an inconvenience for the skunks, of course, but the worst part was that we knew we had totally gassed them out. It crossed our minds that if any of the skunks got mixed up with a Grizzly in the future, they might rush to the haven of our outhouse, knowing full well that its weapons of gas destruction (WGD) were far more powerful than anything a skunk could muster on its own.

Another Twenty Feet

~~~~~~~~~~

Camping out, for people who grew up in the city, can often be confused with setting up a tent in a tree-infested parking lot with shower and bathroom facilities. Sometimes there is even a general store and a laundromat. But it's nothing like you see on the Discovery Channel where adventurous nature lovers camp on mountains, in the Amazon rainforest, or deep inside caves in Montana.

Before I was married I decided to go camping with a bunch of other guys, if you could call it camping, in one of these "wooded motels" in the wild woods of Maine. Here we would have real wild animals to contend with, at least an errant squirrel or chipmunk. We anticipated a 'guys weekend of freedom' where we could just goof off and drink—without the criticism of our significant others for 'being pigs'.

The fun consisted of unloading a trunk, pitching a tent, setting up lawn chairs, cranking up the radio, and pretty much ignoring or defeating everything Mother Nature had to offer. We were young, dumb, and macho and our entertainment came in the form of gobbling food and guzzling drink while swatting mosquitoes. For the life of me, it makes no sense at all now. But for some reason, back then it seemed great.

Bowlful of Laughs

Work details were appointed as a couple of us set up the tents, someone gathered firewood, and another located a water source (which was the outdoor faucet by the general store where we checked in and bought supplies). No doubt the couple who ran this store had a nice little apartment upstairs with a real kitchen, a TV, and comfortable beds.

Not far away, maybe a hundred feet or so across the neatly mown lawn surrounding the general store, were latrines and shower stalls that would have been no surprise in a WWI movie. It was like upscale low-income housing. Bare light bulbs hung on old-style braided wire from a high open-beam ceiling and cement covered the floor. Each toilet stall featured a slatted wooden door in various states of disrepair. Some could close and even latch, but others were held on by noisy rusted one-screw hinges and you had to hold the door shut with some part of your body while using the facilities.

Artistic graffiti adorned the cinder block walls with misspelled four letter words indicating no great intellect. I'd seen better bathrooms in gas stations where the door key was attached to a table leg. It was also a place where you wouldn't want to linger, because the moment the light went on the mosquitoes flooded in. You could quickly lose a pint of blood if you didn't do your business and run for it.

Fortunately, our campsite was fairly isolated from any other campers, so back at the campsite the first bottle was cracked open within an hour or so of arrival and the party was soon in full swing, some of us enjoying a beer or two, some enjoying many. By sundown the steaks were charring nicely and the tin foil wrapped corn-on-the-cob around the edges of the grill was gurgling in the butter inside their cocoons. Each of us had at least one culinary talent that worked even in such rustic surroundings, so though we were a bit lubricated, we managed to put together a passable feast including steaks, salad, mac and cheese, twenty bags of quickly disappearing chips, baked potatoes, and fresh strawberries with whipped cream, all washed down with more beer. We were roughing it and we felt like real men. The only thing missing was the air conditioning.

Mesmerized by the blazing fire and blind to the beauty surrounding us, we took turns recounting stories of our past that took place in the city. We didn't allow the trees or the fresh air to distract us at all as we partied until the wee hours. Finally, bleary-eyed, we packed it in for the night. We separated into the two pop-up tents we had pitched precariously, groggily unfurled our sleeping bags and crawled inside, without a thought that we were sharing the world of genuinely wild animals for the first time in our lives.

The hours of our loud conversation, blasting radio music, and hooting laughter had likely caused anything 4-footed to run for the hills, but with the onset of darkness, the sudden calm may have opened the situation up to furry curiosity. In succumbing to our alcohol-induced comas, we hadn't cleaned up at all. We hadn't thought of putting the food away or suspending it from a high tree branch as wise campers are taught, but simply left everything on the picnic table where we ate, just as if it were our own back yard. Somewhere in our foggy brains, we probably just took for granted that animals were scared of people and that was that.

Somewhere around 3 a.m., Joey sat bolt upright and announced he had to go to the bathroom—bad, and now.

"Anybody else coming?" he asked. Much to his dismay, almost no one woke up, and no one even answered him. He was on his own. He had consumed a huge amount of food and drink and now it was time for the end result. He wasted no time unzipping the tent and vanished at a trot on the wooded path toward the latrines on the other side of the parking lot. Not long afterward I had the vague recollection of the sound of a tent zipper as he returned and climbed back into his sleeping bag. All was quiet again until morning.

The next day, cringing in our tents and squinting against the bright outdoor light, we were up at the crack of Noon—and found everything, food and all, just where we left it. It was no surprise to us city boys. The fire had died out on its own and the place looked pretty much like the disaster area we left behind. It slowly dawned on us in our sobriety how much work getting back to nature involved. The fun aspect had turned to work and the cute homemaking talents we jeered at in our girlfriends suddenly seemed so appealing in their absence.

All in the name of delaying the inevitable cleanup, we decided to shower and wash up before returning to salvage what we could. Joey headed off ahead and the remaining four of us gathered up our toothpastes and soap, and with towels in hand, we trudged slowly off to the showers and latrines. About halfway through the dirt parking lot we stopped dead in our tracks as we stared down at the ground before us. Some dog as big as a bear had apparently defecated right in the parking lot sometime during the night—while we slept nearby in our paper-thin tents without a care in the world.

Another Twenty Feet

Our thoughts turned to all the food and wrappers we had left outside and the realization that this 'dog' had berries in his poop, how likely was that? And then the light began to dawn on us. Only thin canvas and 15 feet separated us from the leftovers and food debris near the grill. We grew somber and began to cast our eyes about suspiciously, wondering what might be the large berry-eating creature that wasn't a dog…

Bowlful of Laughs

We tried to appear confident to each other, but none of
us had ever come this close to an encounter with a wild ani-
mal and we began to entertain some possibilities—what if
some monster Grizzly was stalking us – worse, watching us
from the woods at that very moment. 'What if it was a man-
eater?' the question was posed quietly. Camp observers might
have thought, as we stood there whispering soberly around
that parking lot poop-dump, that we were holding some
kind of a pagan ceremony. No one made a move toward the
latrines as we glanced anxiously back toward our campground.

The sound of laughter can deflate just about anything. And there was an observer - Joey striding back down
the hill from the showers guffawing, having overheard the
"man-eater" remark. He had started out chuckling, and then
began snorting loudly as we turned in his direction. Bears
were no laughing matter, yet our ignorant young friend
found something terribly funny here. By now he had arrived
where we were and was almost doubled-over with laughter
and barely able to talk.

We strained to understand him as he howled and pointed
to the huge dump. Finally he gasped something out between
yuks and hee haws, and even then it was in broken speech. It
sounded like "...another twenty feet... and I woulda made
it...." and we began looking from one to another.

Was he for real? Was he saying what we thought he
was saying?

Apparently when our drunk little camping partner had
dashed out of his tent for the bathroom the night before,
he tripped and fell in the parking lot. And well... he had an

accident of major proportions. Focusing on breaking his fall, he lost his concentration–and nearly his consciousness. And things—everything in fact—got away from him for an instant. And that's all the time it takes in such situations. He never made it to the latrines, he just made it right there... where we were standing.

So here was proof of two old sayings—that "For every action there's an equal and opposite reaction," and that, yes, bears really do 'go in the woods', not in parking lots.

The Victory Lap

~~~~~~~~~~~

My friend Paul and his new wife Lucy were going to the NASCAR races over a long weekend with another couple of newlyweds, Rob and Kathy. We declined to go along because our three small kids wouldn't allow it and only later found out what we had missed.

The four of them were renting one of those gigantic 30-foot recreational vehicles that looks like a movie theatre. It was the deluxe model with all the comforts of home except a fireplace and a pool table. It had an exotic name like "F22 Raptor" or "Detroit Hellcat", but it sucked gas and moved like a box turtle. I figured the fuel bill would likely be amazing.

It was the July 4th weekend, so they would at least have efficient air conditioning, a well-equipped kitchen, two queen-size foldout beds, wall-to-wall carpeting, and sur-round-sound with speaker controls in each bedroom. They also had the thing no one can brag about in a trailer–the typical trailer bathroom, which is usually the only serious drawback of trailer life.

The toilet worked pretty much like any garden variety toilet, only you had to turn a spigot before and after each flush. It also required an additional flush or two to fully dis-pose of its contents into the onboard septic tank, which like

37

any tank, had a maximum capacity and required periodic emptying or evil things could happen. Above the spigot was a quaint little sign reminding the user which way to turn the thing: "Righty-tighty, Lefty-Loosey." The purpose of turning it to "righty" was a moving issue, to assure there was no water in the bowl to splash about when changing lanes on the freeway.

Toilets and traffic are two words that should never appear in the same sentence. They both deal with necessary evils, but that's where the similarity ends. The general consensus was that if someone were daring enough to 'relieve themselves' while the pilot of a super-sized trailer was whipping it along through highway traffic, they were taking their fate into their own hands. There's a time and place for everything, and trust me, a place like the Schuylkill Expressway is one place you do not want to attempt any toilet acrobatics.

Since both couples were without children, life was just one big adventure that began every Friday night and ended every Sunday night, with those pesky five days of work in between as a bothersome interruption. Rob and Kathy's marriage was already experiencing a little "volatility", so Paul and Lucy were getting a little 'relationship education'. Once the trip started, there were a few unpleasant outbursts between them every so often, ranging from minor disagreements to a few near fisticuffs. But they were young and were still working things out.

Paul and Lucy were inclined to just remain silent when tempers flared, waiting a respectable amount of time and then changing the subject to a topic everyone enjoyed, like vacation food and libation. The actual subject of race cars was carefully avoided once it became clear that Kathy already abhorred the idea and didn't consider that entertainment in the first place. An early 'environmentalist', she took every opportunity to comment that 'watching little cars spewing clouds of jet fuel while driving loudly around in circles was less exciting than 'watching a record player idling'. She confessed she'd much rather be on a beach somewhere reading a steamy love novel with the sound and smell of surf in the background. Thus, discussions of drivers and cars and race outcomes were reserved for when Kathy was occupied elsewhere.

The three-day weekend began Friday when they rented out "Moby Van, the White RV," and consumed three days and two nights. Paul and Rob produced their driver's licenses at the trailer rental office, signed the papers, and were given the "walk around," consisting of operating instructions for the various RV contraptions inside and out. The elderly trailer guy said he must have rented out a thousand RV's that performed flawlessly, adding cute little jokes along the way.

He began at the top, discussing the air conditioning, the sound system, the firm mattresses, the range, the refrigerator, all the conveniences, and worked his way down to how to check the oil, use the fire extinguisher, locate the tool box, the flares, operate the toilet, and tend the septic tank.

'When returned Sunday evening,' he said, 'the fuel tank should be full and the septic tank should be empty' or extra charges would apply ($120 if the septic tank was not empty). He explained there were places to empty the tank at various locations, usually behind gas stations touting "RV Facilities" signs. He described how to unfurl a fire hose-like regurgitation pipe with steel fittings that clamped onto the waste receptacle, similar to how jet planes refuel. Paul and Rob nodded casually. It seemed simple enough.

But with excitement in the air, this information went in one ear and out the other faster than the Lowenbrau Porsche. The little band had bigger fish to fry, like cramming all their food provisions into the tiny onboard 4-cubic foot fridge; three days worth of groceries for four people on vacation is a lot of food.

In addition, they were bringing a king-sized cooler to accommodate all the shrimp, steaks, chili, salmon, burgers, corn-on-the-cob, peach cobbler, snacks, and eight or nine cases of beer to wash everything down. The first fly in the ointment was halfway to their destination when they realized they underestimated on their purchase of toilet paper supplies. But the trip to the track was otherwise uneventful.

Paul parked the RV in the infield within the somewhat circular race track, only later finding out it was considered the rowdy section where some race attendees actually lived on the brink of consciousness, forming unruly bands that roved the expanse at night and during the day were blind to the stock cars racing around them at speeds in excess of 200 MPH. The clicking of beer cans snapping open, combined with raw Detroit horsepower, lent an air of bravery and recklessness to the event.

A ladder on the rear of the RV provided access to its roof from where the couples viewed most of the races in lawn chairs up on top. Paul, Lucy, and Rob sat there in the sun, beers in hand, watching the stock cars tear by on the one unobstructed section of track they could see. But the novelty quickly wore off. The conversation, which consisted mostly of shouting above the roar of engines, soon turned to food. Kathy, reveling in her misery inside the RV, was conspicuously missing during all of this.

I think it was Benjamin Franklin who said "Company is like fish - they begin to stink in a few days". And so it was that these four, confined to the RV together, soon began wondering who thought up the term 'recreational vehicle' when 'a cage on wheels' would have made more sense. They were all getting on each other's nerves, until they lived just to survive the day, the high point of which was dinner. And to avoid biting each other's heads off, everyone invested heavily in this event, eating hearty like at a shark feeding frenzy.

But the downside was that the septic tank was quickly filling up, and then other avenues involving port-o-potties had to be located, which only fueled the angst. Sunday afternoon was the final race, followed by the victory lap for the NASCAR race winner after the race was over. The weekend was drawing to a close, and not a moment too soon.

The parade of RVs and pickups-with-cabs-over began the slow "Head for Home waltz" from the camping area. It was a good hour in line before the place emptied out and the four relieved RV prisoners were rolling down the open road headed south towards Philly to return their rolling behemoth. In the silence, all hoped they could just call it a weekend and still part as friends.

Closing in on the home stretch after filling up the gas, Paul suddenly remembered they still had to empty the dang septic tank or pay the $120 fee. Groaning and whining, the strung out little group was already pushed to their limit, and now they realized they had about 60 gallons of raw sewage onboard to dispose of. The going service charge for its disposal was $1 a gallon and it seemed like a lousy waste of money, especially with their funds about exhausted and now they might have to forego dinner. Their brains began racing to come up with an alternative.

Now today, no one in their right mind would consider dumping sewage anywhere other than where it should be dumped, but back then things were a little looser and most people didn't even know what environmental ecology was. In Arlo Guthrie's song Alice's Restaurant, he sings "We saw another pile of garbage at the bottom of a hill and we decided that one big pile was better than two small piles, so rather then bring that one up, we decided to throw ours down." That was the cavalier philosophy that guided the thinking of the time. And yeah, saving sixty bucks definitely trumped trashing the environment.

We've all done things we've regretted and the by-now-not-so-merry band of four were about to do something they'd surely regret and pay for dearly in karma. Sixty gallons of raw sewage is not something to just be swept under the rug.

Someone suggested that a residential construction site would work, and since it was Sunday, no one would be around. Finding a foundation trench shouldn't be too difficult, right? There were piles of dirt there, stacks of debris, rocks, stones, and bricks. In a few days it might sink into the ground, or even evaporate, right? Or if discovered, it might provoke a few laughs. They could almost make it sound reasonable if they kept trying.

The object was to drive in, dump the tank, and get out. This had to be carried out with the same clandestine efficiency as a bank robbery, so they put their heads together and planned the execution of the deed, going over every detail; the approach, the unfurling of the long unwieldy heavy-duty hose, firing up the auxiliary generator, switching the valves to "open" and the final expulsion of said waste material. Then came the recoiling of the hose and, of course, the getaway, which would be the "victory lap", their "victory lap", signifying the end of their glorious adventure and looking forward to the evening's sixty dollar dinner together.

A large sign loomed ahead advertising "Forest Acres". It sounded like a pleasant, out of the way spot, so they got off the turnpike and headed off into the hills of Pennsylvania where the affluent would someday be mowing lawns and cultivating gardens as school buses gathered or dropped off little ones. What harm could a little "fertilizer" do? They navigated down what was, for now, a ghost town, with little but paved streets and skeletons of houses framed out in various stages of completion. They couldn't have asked for a better location.

They parked the RV about 50 feet past a bulldozer at the top of a small hill, figuring everything normally rolls downhill anyway, so why fight fate? All went as planned until it came time for the actual "dirty deed" of squirting the tank contents from the eight-inch diameter hose. The hose proved to be much heavier than expected. Once the contents filled the hose, it would be heavier still, a snag they hadn't counted on. Further, the open end of the hose had a steel clamping device that indicated a certain amount of pressure and restraint might be required to control it. As their minds raced, they exchanged glances in a moment of stunned silence.

Paul and Rob went towards the rear to the auxiliary motor on the side of the RV and re-read the instructions; which valves to turn to pump out the sewage. They were stalling and everybody knew it. Finally, Kathy, always the feisty one, stepped up to the plate, grabbed the heavy hose, aimed it down the hill and yelled "fire away!"

The hose nozzle was pointed properly, so Paul and Rob wasted no time. The 10 HP engine roared to life, the valves were opened, and all hell broke loose–for about 4 seconds. The raw liquid sewage shot out a few feet, but then slowed to a crawl when the lumpier, more solid material began to exit. Clearly more pressure was needed.

But before anyone could decide how to proceed, the motor automatically revved up to move the heavier sludge through the bulging hose; so much, in fact, that it became abundantly clear why there was a steel clamping device on the end of the hose. This pressure was nothing that any mortal man, or woman, could control, let alone aim free-lance.

Like a twenty-foot anaconda, the hose came alive and began whipping around in dangerous and disgusting gyrations with Kathy in tow, several times lifting her slight frame 8-10 feet off the ground and tossing her this way and

45

that while she clung to it with a vengeance (while screaming like a Banshee for backup); but the others—frozen in
shock—could only watch helplessly.

Then Kathy flinched, and no one blamed her. She had
to let go and dropped to the ground in a pitiful heap, and
then managed to get to her feet, recognize her plight, and
make a run for it. The other three suddenly realized they
had missed their chance and should have helped, because
now they too had become its target. They had no choice but
to try to outrun this 'fountain from hell' spewing a heavy
spray of raw filth for fifty feet in every direction. They also
bolted, but too late–there was no escape.

Kathy finally got up the hill to the far side of the
RV just behind the other three. That was about when the
hose shot straight up like a circus elephant's trunk, completely dousing everything within a half mile, including the
RV itself, and coating all of them, as well as the doors and
windows, with a foamy brown liquid. The stench defied
description and the same thoughts were running through
everyone's minds—how much was sixty gallons? How long
would this last? If the average car holds about twenty gallons of gas, they had most of this nightmarish performance
still to witness. The tension was palpable.

By the time the sewage tank was close to empty and
the hose lay still undulating on the ground like a writhing
python, the "filthy four" were covered in a slick of excre-
ment and smelling like sewer rats. They couldn't even look
at each other. The only good thing, if you could call it good,
was that no-one could blame anyone else for the outcome—

they were all equally complicit. A glance at the RV revealed even the door handles they needed to grasp to get inside to their clean clothes were coated in sewage.

And the final insult was having to have the RV washed before finally returning it. Cost? Seventy-five dollars. The moral of the story you can guess for yourself, lest I be forced to use dirty language to describe the metaphor. OK, I'll just say it—grime doesn't pay!

Scumcroft

~~~~~~~~~~~

One of my favorite roommating experiences was when I was living at the bottom of the top of the barrel in Bala Cynwyd, Pennsylvania off City Line Avenue. Immediately west of Philadelphia, railroad barons of yesteryear settled here and built some of the most exquisite posh mansions in the country along Route 30 toward Lancaster and the Pennsylvania Dutch area. This was Lancaster Avenue—the Main Line, the upper crust; established wealth, butlers and maids, manicured lawns, statues of little boys on pedestals peeing into marble ponds, and Bentleys in the driveways.

Our coveted rental house was an old Queen Anne Victorian we nicknamed 'Scumcroft', a ginger-bread-decked, built-like-a-brick (or so we thought) house that had been abandoned in 1933 for reasons unknown. The place had been boarded up and left for dead long ago, until an enterprising young carpenter bought it, fixed it up, and converted it into a 'wannabe-Happy-Hippie-home' some years later. He created a master suite for himself downstairs and rented the upstairs out to three transients; each got a large individual bedroom and use of a communal bathroom. I was one of those transients.

Scumcroft

The house stood out like a hearse at a home game—there was litter everywhere. We had old wheel-less cars up on cinder blocks, two-foot tall grass, and our best efforts to keep the place up just fell flat. We were all just working class heroes, the bluest of blue collars.

Our bathroom, strategically located up on the second floor, had a broken window pane (we taped cardboard over it in the winter) and a busted shade. A bare 150-watt light bulb lit up the tiny room like a floodlight and hung so low you always hit your head when using the facilities, causing it to swing wildly back and forth casting bizarre shadows about. The view from outside the house at night was reminiscent of peering upward toward the torture chamber in the silent black and white horror movie classic, The Cabinet of Dr. Caligari.

In the remodeling process, the new owner arbitrarily knocked down a few supporting walls and built others, 'fixed' the furnace, cleaned up the yard and planted shrubs, and then discovered the well-established termite infestation that must have emptied the place originally. And if termites have a military system, these were now well-trained Green Berets. They had colonized an area that may have consisted of the entire bowels of the house. The sage exterminators the owner had called in had one word of rare wisdom: "Move." But by then, it was too late. It was already rented out and making him money.

Fortunately we rarely saw these pests because they had tunneled far into depths of the foundation. Basically we had a pact; we left them alone and they left us alone. 'Live and let eat wood', we all decided.

Aside from the balsa holding the place up, the only evidence we'd ever see or hear of the millions of winged tenants downstairs was in the spring when termites swarm. The walls literally vibrated and buzzed in the dining room. Fear kept us out, but morbid curiosity would draw us back. By the time I moved in, it was common knowledge that anyone could poke a finger right through the thick wooden beams in the basement (and possibly the above ground frame wood behind the wallboard). The heater boiler was cracked worse than the people who paid money to live here, and to have any heat at all, the old heating system had to be abandoned for the more common radiators we see today.

Steam radiators, when working properly, are much hotter than conventional radiators. But these original-looking steam jobs were also different than normal steam radiators—they had long, nasty-looking spikes all over them designed to radiate heat or kill whoever accidentally touched them. The inventor of these steam radiators was no doubt tarred, feathered, and promptly sent out of town on the next bus. Today, these monstrosities would certainly be outlawed by building safety codes.

Steam engines and boilers worked well in boats and locomotives, but not in things that remained stationary. It had something to do with the tremendous pressure they could generate. They were invaluable during the Industrial Revolution, with one small problem; steam engines tended to blow up occasionally. They not only put some towns on the map, but took some off as well.

In our case, the cracked boiler was less of an explosion-hazard than an inconvenience. It just meant some unlucky soul had to periodically go down into the dungeon-like basement and turn a spigot until the sight glass on the boiler filled up. The sight glass was a clear glass test tube-looking thing that gradually filled up with water after you turned the water spigot on.

All things being equal, the water eventually reached the top of the tube in anywhere from six to fifteen minutes (depending on if someone were in the shower or not). Then we'd turn the spigot back off. Under original operating conditions, if the boiler spigot were not shut off in time, they'd likely find a crater, and maybe a toilet seat, where the house once stood. Pretty simple, huh? Well, not so much at 2:45 a.m. when you were half asleep and it was your turn to do boiler duty. You'd be surprised how many times we'd all forget which way to turn the blasted thing to shut the water off.

The original plumber was likely dyslexic. Hot and cold piping was inconsistent throughout the plumbing/heating system and was never relegated to specific left or right positions. Clockwise and counter-clockwise were mixed up throughout as well. Nobody knew who the plumber was, only that he was a musician named "Cross eyed-Pete-the-Cyclops." We think he was put on a bus out of town too, possibly for Nashville.

This little matter of the cracked boiler was rarely disclosed to new renters until after they had moved in. Nobody told us—why should we tell them?

We'd wait a day or two and when we were all hanging out together, one of our veterans would cheerfully jump up and proclaim it was his or her turn "to do the boiler." The new recruit's ears would perk up and curiosity always brought up the rear. Historically it worked like gangbusters every time. It was our little game.

Every few months or so, when the cockamamie boiler would quit altogether, we'd have no choice but to call a repairman. To actually fix the ancient thing they would have had to call a guy out of retirement, but it wasn't really fixable—these were just band aid calls. Invariably they'd send a different guy each time, someone completely unfamiliar with one of these relics, so the repairman rarely saw this as a "small matter". I can't remember how many times we went through the drill. First we'd hear a surprise exclamation from the cellar, then cursing, followed by an awed silence, then full-blown panic. The repair guy would come charging up the stairs at a dead run, sweat streaming down his forehead, screaming "The boiler's cracked! She's gonna blow! Run for your lives!" It was kinda like Scotty in Star Trek.

We'd just calm the guy down and tell him to throw in a can of the same stuff the last repairman dumped into the boiler. He'd blink his eyes as if waking up from hibernation, lope out to his truck and get a can of that stuff that had pictures of snakes and gears on the outside and pour it in, hand us the bill, leave, and we'd throw the bill in the trash. We had it down pat.

The upstairs bathroom was a different problem altogether. For the most part the sink and tub behaved, but that toilet had it in for us. It was over the living room and wouldn't you know, it had an annoying leak that dribbled down through the floor right smack in front of the television set downstairs. If it were raining in the movie we were watching, this actually added to the drama of the flick, but how often did that happen?

I finally fixed the problem myself. Well, half the problem anyway. This leak created a nasty puddle in front of the TV that dang near got a few of us electrocuted as we reached to turn the thing on or change the channel. Once Dermitt got up to put the news on at eleven and zap! He developed an annoying tic on the right side of his face after that and his hair was never the same. Luckily we never had a fatality, just a lot of food stains on the ceiling and the corner walls when people slipped in the puddle and did a "cow pasture slide" carrying a plate of spaghetti. I cured the puddle problem, not the leak, by making a hole in the floor with a nail the size of a railroad spike exactly where the water drops hit the floor. Call it mind expansion, I don't know. I hate to brag.

The worst problem with the toilet was when the boiler had leaked its total contents. The whole plumbing system was tied together and whenever the boiler ran dry, so did the toilet. A bone dry toilet wasn't very inviting when you needed it because this meant a right-now trip down a couple flights to the basement to turn the spigot to replenish the system and refill the toilet—which took a while. To a "last minute person" this could spell disaster. Having a bowel movement under these conditions was actually an operation similar to what a crew must go through to submerge or surface a submarine. You could almost hear the "Oogah–oogah" alarm in your mind as you waited in the basement with crossed legs (or worse) for the boiler to fill up and then the toilet.

56

Scumcroft

Nowadays houses usually feature two toilets, but not Scumcroft. My dog had fewer problems than we did. He would push open the screen door to let himself out, do his business leisurely, and even managed to open the door afterward to get back in. Meanwhile, we were running up and down stairs, turning spigots, dancing and cursing, and hoping nobody else would jump in line ahead of us while we were in the basement pulling levers, doing setup operations, and watching the sight glass.

Going to the bathroom in Scumcroft required planning, skill, agility (narrow staircase and wobbly banister), and above all, speed. Once you'd performed all the technical duties required and made it back up two flights of stairs to the bathroom, if the door was closed and someone else was seated on the throne, there was little recourse beyond just holding tight and exchanging colorful words.

Problems during the morning rush were only avoided through careful timing and strict schedules, but these schedules left little room for error. Whoever overslept was automatically bumped to the end of the procession and inevitably got to work late. Weekend parties, on the other hand, posed a much larger problem, as a keg of beer can cause the release of liquid faster than our toilet could process the output, and our personal elimination systems far outpaced that of the plumbing.

While the night was still young, the bathroom quickly bottlenecked and as a result the backyard would get well "watered". The more frequent the parties, the more our lawn remained a sickly yellow, and our acceptability in the neighborhood took another nose dive. (Everyone blamed my dog, but any sane person knew it would take a dog the size of Babe the Blue Ox to accomplish that coverage – not to mention it all happened out in plain sight. When you've had a few beers, you're sure no one has any idea what's going on but you, even when a large crowd has gathered.)

Then one day a piece of paper was nailed to the front door informing us of the news that our beloved Scumcroft had been condemned. Big surprise! It was scheduled to be demolished and replaced with a real house. We had three months to vacate our quirky little commune—and fate-tempter that I was, I was the last to depart. As places (and roommates) go, it was hard to give up the youthful camaraderie, and houses can get pretty spooky when the living leave. The last few months I was a little lonely with just the dog, but happily, at least the toilet was eventually all mine. I was the captain in sole charge of the ship.

My remaining days there were less hectic, and my stress levels returned to just about normal. A couple of weeks after I moved out, I drove past the place—now a vacant lot—and it was totally deserted. I couldn't help but notice the grass looked a lot better, and there was a lone port-o-potty in the backyard. Dang! Why hadn't we thought of that?

Go With the Flow

~~~~~~~~~~~

One of my more intriguing adventures occurred while renting a decrepit two room apartment in a dilapidated tenement in Philadelphia's *Queen Village*. This was where Benjamin Franklin originally set foot which lent an amusing and historical element to the neighborhood. I shared the place with my faithful mutt George who, by inheritance, represented every other dog that ever lived in that city.

The ten-foot ceiling imparted a palatial effect despite the steady stream of plaster debris that rained on our heads whenever the 2nd Street Bus roared by. The bathroom ceiling, in particular, looked as if it had been ravaged by some exotic plaster disease. Every attempt to repair it, both amateur and professional, had failed miserably.

It wasn't much but for George and me it was our paradise, our Shangri la. As long as we didn't look up everything was fine. That all changed one day, however.

One day, while seated upon the toilet, I was rudely interrupted. You could say I was "clearing my thoughts" or "minding my own business" when a large drop of cold water landed squarely on top of my head. Something like this had never happened to me at such an intimate moment and I felt my privacy had been deliberately violated. I had no idea

who or what was to blame but I vowed revenge; someone
would pay.

I pulled myself together and leaped from my seat (as
much as one can at a time like this) just as the next perfectly
timed drop fell from above and plopped directly into the
toilet with deadly accuracy. It could have hit the toilet seat
or the floor nearby but instead it chose to land right smack
in the middle of the bowl, making a perfect drip sound
"*Boyt!*" Amazing. Robin Hood couldn't have done this any
better with bow and arrow.

Eyes wide and captivated by this thrilling event,
George and I strained our necks and stared at the crack
in the ceiling. The dripping sped up and began running
quite freely, and as always, the drops fell ten feet straight
down and landed smack dab in the center of my toilet bowl.
"*Boyt! Boyt! Boyt!*" But after a few minutes it slowed down
and stopped altogether, which somehow seemed to fuel the
puzzle.

How likely was it for a water leak in the upstairs
plumbing to snake its way through walls and floors and
then manage to deliver this renegade dribble precisely into
another toilet after a daring ten foot leap? This was incred-
ible. *Was this an intelligent life force?*

Over time, the water show continued on and off and
through all hours of the day and night, but since the water
never wound up on the floor I never hit the panic button
and just made sure the toilet remained open so things could
go on uninterrupted. For reasons of his own, George agreed
with the plan and felt a toilet with the seat up was far more

valuable than a toilet with the seat down, therefore the decision was unanimous and ratified on the spot. We could never see eye-to-eye on the exact purpose of the toilet but, regardless, we agreed it did make sense to use the facility quickly and get out of the way.

L. Webb

Bowlful of Laughs

All was well for a couple of weeks until one evening when, again, I heard the well-known *"ker-plop"* coming from the bathroom: *"Boyt! Boyt! Boyt Boyt Boyt!"* This time, though, the unrelenting beat seemed to suggest something sinister was in store. Louder than usual, every drop had an ominous ring to it. George noticed this too and he came to my side.

My hunch was correct and soon the water gained a driving force that had taken on a deliberate, menacing flow as if someone had turned on a faucet up in my ceiling. Luckily, the aim was still dead on, but now the water's might was causing considerable "splashage" onto the surrounding floor. The water magically appeared from the ceiling and just as quickly it vanished into the toilet below: *Hello!- Goodbye! Who'd believe such a thing?*

George and I fixed our eyes on the ceiling. We knew things were out of control and could get worse at any moment even though we weren't sure how. We looked at each other. We looked at the crack in the ceiling. We looked at the toilet. We looked at each other again. We gulped, we blinked. George had never seen such a thing either and he wanted answers too. Some primitive instinct stirred and I could see the wheels turning in his head. His upper lip began to quiver and he emitted a low growl and readied himself to attack.

The enormity of the situation had escalated and now the surge inside the toilet was beyond high tide and the approaching flood waters were a fact. *Could the whole ceiling fall down?*

Go With the Flow

I ordered George to keep an eye on things, gave the toilet one last flush, and ran upstairs where I began pounding on the door of the apartment directly above mine. There was no answer but I kept on pounding and shouting anyway. "There's a flood downstairs, open up!" Finally, the door slowly swung open and I was met by a sleepy-eyed old man in a terrycloth bathrobe who mumbled something about an "overflowing bathtub." I instantly recalled the hundred times this had happened before and felt my own hackles rising. He absently closed the door in my face and a few seconds later I heard screeching spigots slowly closing as if there was no hurry.

I returned downstairs to find George still on guard but now his head tilted to one side and his fierce growl ended on a high note, almost musical. The waterfall had dwindled to a drizzle then stopped altogether, but at least now the mystery was solved. For one crazy moment I wondered if I had imagined the whole thing until one single tell-tale drop brought me back to reality. *"Boyt!"*

The damage had been done—there had been a small flood that was now draining into the floor boards. Rather than sop it up with a towel, we decided to go outside, get some air, clear our heads, take a walk and let George to do some sprinkling of his own.

As George and I came back from our walk around the block, we bumped into our neighbor, Jacques, the French chef who lived directly below us. He was pacing on the sidewalk in front of his apartment. The door to his place was wide open. I had never seen him in such a state. His hair was roughed up, his face was red, and he appeared to be walking in tight circles as he talked to himself and made wild gyrations with his arms.

Famous for his lavish parties, the French chef entertained often. Many times his parties lasted into the wee hours as the aroma of fancy dishes with names no one could pronounce, served up with exotic wines, wafted through the neighborhood. Exotic jazz, we had all come to appreciate, danced through the walls. Today, however, the suave chef had completely "lost it."

Before I had a chance to relay my story of the water theme park in my bathroom and "Bathtub Bob's" involvement, Jacques interrupted and, in broken English, began to spew out his own soggy calamity. From what I gathered, he had been entertaining when some kind of flood "spewed forth from above" that had ruined the festivities. *"Sacré Bleu!"* he croaked, fuming. He motioned for me to follow him inside.

We took the invite graciously and George led the way. Once inside, George took advantage of the open door to the basement and vanished into uncharted territory, or should I say "waters?"

There was water everywhere–and soaking his ornate dining table. The stage was set for company—a white damask tablecloth set with Paul Revere silver, bouquets of flowers, and candelabra on either end displaying gigantic and elegantly carved candles. The center was reserved for his signature creation, *Goose Flambé a la Shallot.*

At first, Jacques seemed equally amazed with the water's path and aim as he was injured by the injustices it had caused. He pointed to the evil orifice on the ceiling where the water had first teasingly trickled before turning into a raging tsunami. From there, the waves targeted, and then drenched the table with a vengeance not seen since Russia stopped Napoleon in 1812.

Chef Jacques had painstakingly whisked, mixed, beat and then tenderly coaxed his top secret concoction to rise nearly a foot in an oven set at precisely 329 degrees Fahrenheit. Eighteen minutes and five seconds later, his inflated creation was moved from oven to table beside the flowers, bathed in cognac, then volcanically ignited between the elegant candles, reminiscent of the south bank of Kilauea, illuminating the delighted faces of his influential company.

A two minute pyrotechnic display was the intended main event of the evening's splendiferous meal, but within seconds a curtain of water descended through the ceiling onto the flaming centerpiece, extinguishing the flames and the candlelight and drowning the poor goose in a cloud of hissing steam. The goose imploded and toppled to starboard with the sound of a deflating whoopee cushion.

Apparently, the good chef had been entertaining an important group of restaurateurs from New York, along with an imminent career change, when the dam broke and the flood waters rose. Jacques' tirade continued as these great injustices came to light; first, the flood, then the fizzled fireworks, and worst of all, his important guests fleeing like scared rabbits and getting out of Dodge, leaving him only with a roomful of overturned chairs and a platter of deflated paté.

With a trembling hand, and as the final blow, Chef Jacques produced an old wrinkled photo of his famous *Goose Flambé* and how his undisputed masterpiece appeared in its unmolested state. Just above the bird was a billowing white banner with the word *"Voila!"* printed in gold.

The colorful photo displayed a graceful longneck goose in a rare pose that suggested flight. Perched in an antique bone-white casserole dish with a wide oval lip, the bird was landing in an almost fluorescent turquoise liquid containing what appeared to be pond weed or lily pads surrounded with delicate white lotus blossoms garnishing the perimeter. The dish framing the goose bore an unmistakable resemblance to a toilet seat and I immediately realized Bathtub Bob's clever water had seen this as such, couldn't resist, and dove right in.

Without turning his head, Jacques slowly raised his arm and pointed to what was left of his artwork. He couldn't bear to look. Voice cracking and with a tear in one eye, he tenderly recounted how his desperate attempts of resuscitation proved fatal as the massive avian succumbed to its death throes on the operating table and the goose's head fell off. There, in all its agony, lay his drowned *pièce de résistance*, a huge bird-like form made of glazed pâté, resting in two pieces in its coffin of ornate cut glass. We observed a moment of silence.

Chef Jacques pointed toward the doorway that led to the basement. He explained that in the height of this mêlée he suddenly remembered that his real treasure sat unprotected in the basement below. Fortunately, his panic was

66

replaced with calm after discovering the wicked water had missed its mark by a yard. By virtue of a simple wrong turn, the nearsighted stream sought what it perceived as a toilet seat and invaded an old snow tire by mistake. *Aha! Now I felt I knew the beast.*

As we descended into the basement, a myriad of paintings came into view. Stacked about as far as the eye could see, there were paintings of all shapes and sizes. By the time we had reached the bottom of the stairs the quantity was daunting. It seemed that the chef's culinary expertise had blossomed into the realm of visual art.

Unfortunately, his zeal for art outshined his talent and, alas, this was his nemesis. Eager to overcome this disparity, Jacques pounced on every opportunity to gain his due recognition and reverse this dilemma. He seized the moment and launched into a long winded, well rehearsed speech for the sole benefit of me and my dog.

I became claustrophobic and wanted to escape but instead, out of respect, I made polite gestures and kind comments. Lifted by this, Jacques took a deep breath and picked up the pace. Fearing this would go into overtime, I nervously looked around for a rescue. I saw nothing.

Suddenly, his speech stopped and with undue aplomb, he motioned toward his undisputed masterpiece slightly behind him and to his right. Squinting, I tried to make sense of the wild colors exploding in all directions. With *esprit de corps*, Jacques proudly pointed to his mind-bending rendition of an intergalactic waterfall in a distant galaxy. An oval, white nebulous cloud encircled the "meat and potatoes of the painting" forming a familiar image. *Another toilet seat? Uh oh.*

My rescue came in the form of my faithful sidekick, George, a critic in his own right. With the whites of his eyes showing and his nose working overtime, he examined the "intergalactic waterfall" with apparent distaste. I glanced down just in time to see him yawn and lift his leg. *Deplorable manners, but what a critic!*

George knew it was time for us to leave and scampered up the stairway. Hoping the great artist wouldn't notice the ultimate insult, I decided to go with the flow and followed my friend up the stairs and out the door.

Just Can't Hide It

~~~~~~~~~~

S hortly after moving into my new digs in Atlanta for
a job relocation, the dark shadow that has followed
me much of my life again reared its ugly head. I knew it
was only a matter of time before it cropped up again like
a bad penny, and once again I was facing *The Curse of the
Commode.*

I've traveled a lot and used executive bathrooms in
large corporations, grungy bathrooms in gas stations, and
even my share of port-a-potties in everything from work
sites to campgrounds. That said, I must admit it was never
a surprise when I flushed a toilet and saw its contents slug-
gishly rotate clockwise as the water level rose threateningly.
Below the equator the water rotates counter-clockwise, and
I often wondered what affect this might have on the curse.
But that's neither here nor there...or is it?

Curse or not, it had happened again and it was time
to fix the problem (same problem, different facilities). And
although anyone who's had as much trouble with toilets as
I have should have a gold-plated toilet plunger by now, I
was caught short and saw a trip to the local Walmart in my
future.

The cute name for a toilet plunger is a "plumber's
friend." And although there is no more shame in buying

this item than there is in buying toilet paper, an unexplainable embarrassment does exist. Buying a toilet plunger is the same as announcing to the world that you have clogged a toilet, which implies a certain intestinal fortitude similar to a hippopotamus. I only knew a few people in the area, but I knew the way that fate works; if I were ever going to bump into someone I knew, this would be the time. I wore sunglasses.

Making the Buy

I strolled the aisles nonchalantly. I'm a man's man and I don't ask for directions. I passed through housewares, the electronics department, the small appliance section, and auto parts. Forty-five minutes later I was still roaming around when I stumbled over some PVC piping and realized I had actually found plumbing supplies.

Over the years I have developed a sixth sense when it comes to finding toilet plungers, even in the largest department stores that feature everything from tires to washing machines. And even when the longtime employee announces, "We don't carry them," if they are there, I can sense their presence. When I walk through the checkout with my plunger, I wink at them.

But truth be told, there's something terribly demeaning about walking around with a toilet plunger. You'll never find toilet plungers near the Shoe Department in the middle of the store where you could hide it behind rows of boxes. Or in Lawn and Garden where you could make an unobtrusive exit through the outdoor plant section, although they don't exactly make good gifts like a bird feeder.

And you won't find them right near the entrance where you could grab one and get right in line at the cash register. Nope. Plumbing is generally along the back of the store with auto supplies. This way your embarrassment is maximized, because you have to wave the thing around as you navigate your way back to the checkout area six miles away.

Since I found what I came for, I looked around furtively, and when no one was watching I deftly plucked it up and headed for the checkout, swinging it casually in sync with my stride to hide it behind my leg as I walked. So far so good.

I took pains to locate the shortest checkout line, and once in line I remembered how that often backfires when the person up front produces an item without a price or bar code. "Price check on Aisle 5" can turn into an eternity when you're holding a toilet plunger. And sure enough, just like clockwork, the third guy in line had a problem.

The line grew longer as we waited, and waited, and waited. Ultimately it was no use, as people were shifting from foot to foot in boredom and the price check continued ad infinitum. I had the plunger beside me against my leg, but by then everyone was casting about for anything the least bit interesting, and of course someone spotted the plunger. They pointed and whispered.

Then two of them giggled and whispered to a third person. Finally I gave up trying to hide it and threw it over my shoulder like a rifle and began pacing back and forth in line like a Buckingham Palace guard. It was too late - the truth was out. But at least we all got a few laughs out of it.

The gentleman in front of the cash register, a hefty fellow possessed of a rare sense of humor, delivered a well-practiced line he must have loved an occasion to use. He was enjoying my discomfort as I brought the plunger into view at the last possible moment and placed it onto the moving conveyor belt. When it stopped in front of him, the cashier froze and stared at it in all its wood-and-rubber magnificence. He looked at it the way one would look at an AK-47. He gingerly picked it up between his thumb and forefinger and displayed it openly for all to see, then turned to me with a slitty-eyed furtive expression and said in a low voice, "Uh, you got a license for this?"

With my cover blown, I pulled out my wallet and slid my card through the slot we've all come to know and detest. The smiling cashier then got me again. He tied a large fluorescent red warning flag to the handle where it would attract the most attention, and then deftly placed only the head of the plunger in one of those miserably small bags that exposed the entire handle and defeated any possibility of concealing its identity. The bag closed around the plunger head like shrinkwrap, taking on the unmistakable silhouette of the plunger. It was a dead giveaway. The only thing missing was my wearing a bright red T-shirt with flashing metallic lettering saying "I Just Bought a Toilet Plunger."

Naturally my car was at the far end of the parking lot, possibly in another state, so I had to grin and bear it as I

left the store, walking past hundreds of other shoppers, trying to appear casual. But many did stop—and stare, and I
knew what they were thinking. They looked at me and my
plunger in the same way people look at a morbid car accident as they drive by, as if glad it wasn't them.

How Does it Work?

The saying "Build a better mousetrap and the world
will beat a path to your door" leaves one with the impression that mousetraps don't work well. But actually mousetraps work just fine. It's simply mechanics governed by a
compression spring. They'd probably work on elephants if
they made them big enough, or if elephants ever imposed a
threat, which I doubt because they are not that sort.

So how efficient is the common toilet plunger? The
escape hatch in the bottom of the toilet bowl is oval, yet the
rubber plunger is round. What's wrong with this picture?
We're not talking rocket science here. Remember the test
in kindergarten? The square peg and the square hole versus
the round peg and the round hole? Few people have actually failed this test of intellect, but whoever did is probably
the guy that designed the toilet plunger.

And further, why they don't sell raincoats the next aisle
over from toilet plungers is anybody's guess. No matter how
you position the thing, the dreaded splash-back is a fore-
gone conclusion. I've always considered taking a shower to
be the final step in unclogging the toilet.

A shower cap and goggles are also important to have
on hand when giving it the final `old heave-ho'. And it

would probably really help if they made the plunger handle about eight feet long too, but then where would you store it? By the stepladder? Standing up in the garage? But like a rake, if someone stepped on it, would they be maimed for life? Or have to walk around for the rest of their lives with a plunger on their face? This is the type of dilemma best handled by NASA. If they can put a man on the moon, this should be a no-brainer. It's just simple physics, hydraulics, and leverage, right?

Well, ok, maybe not so much. I once read about the Space Shuttle commode and it's true that an entirely different set of dynamics are in play there, involving suction, motors, and what happens when things hit the fan. Even dealing with the commonest of functions, zero gravity presents a whole new slant on the laws of quantum physics, which only gives us one more reason to leave space exploration to the really brave.

Toilets Around the World

I watched a show on the History Channel that was all about toilets, and toward the end they featured the Rolls Royce of toilets, Big Bertha. This toilet could consume 22 golf balls in one swallow, placing it right up there with the many Wonders of the World such as the Sphinx, the Grand Canyon, and Iguazu Falls.

In San Jose I was introduced to the *self-flushing* toilets and urinals that spare you having to touch the handle, but even these modern marvels have been known to go haywire. Having no other way to express themselves, when frustrated they have been known to go on a non-stop flushing spree even when there's nobody in the room. I can tell you, people are reluctant to hop on a hopper while there's a miniature geyser erupting inside. And I can understand that. If it were me, I'd want a fighting chance before getting drenched and dragged down the drain. It made me wonder if other more sophisticated machinery such as Ferris wheels and roller coasters might be prone to similar afflictions.

These *auto-flush* toilets have now spread to restrooms around the country. Add to that the new innovation where the lights turn on as you enter the room and shut off as you leave, and the sink faucets that just 'know' your hands are about to go under them and the water suddenly comes on—at just the right temperature, I might add. The next thing will likely be music speakers in the toilet paper holder while a screen in the stall door shows you the news and weather, and then tells you to peel that piece of toilet paper off your shoe.

But for now, my own toilet was under the weather and me along with it. A man without a toilet is a man without a purpose. It's not as if I hadn't faced this dilemma before, but I often had roommates or family members around for an appreciative audience to encourage me while I was handling the plunger task. And when I had completed it, my audience cheered me as I walked slowly around the bathroom, toilet plunger held high overhead, accepting the accolades. (I only did that once – then I had to wash up and change my clothes after I realized I was being dribbled on with each wave.)

But this time I was on my own with no friendly cheer-leaders, and facing the daunting task of unclogging a strange toilet I'd barely met. If I won, there was no one to celebrate with. If I lost, I was alone with the menace of a clogged toilet, so I couldn't allow myself to even think of defeat.

Getting Down to Business

I knew the secret was to use elbow grease to force water (or whatever might be available in the bowl) down and out through the drain in the bottom of the bowl. We are told that leads directly to the sewer system or septic tank, but since childhood I've had my doubts as to where it really leads. Few people have ever seen the actual destination with their own eyes. Signs above some public toilets read "Flush Twice - it's a Long Way to the Office."

I've also seen *honey dippers*, the trucks that suck septic tanks dry, with signs on the back reading "Full of Politician's Empty Promises." If nothing else, the toilet is the birthplace of apathy. It's hard to care where a clog ends up, as long as it's *out of **here***. I rolled up my sleeves and got to work.

For those of you who are new at this, you might want to take notes. When approaching your own personal clog, you should have a rough idea what you're dealing with. Speaking from experience, it's good to know whether we are talking about just a caboose or an entire locomotive train. If you're unclogging for someone else, don't let their dainty frame fool you—the largest stools can come from some of the smallest fools.

Bowlful of Laughs

Preparations should include an interrogation of each user regarding what their last meal consisted of. Did we have a salad or did we have Wiener Schnitzel and potatoes with a side of dumplings? These things all figure into the mix and let you know what you're up against. I don't mean to get 'down and dirty' here, but we're not talking about flower arrangements now, are we?

A successful plunge is when everything in the bowl suddenly exits all on its own, independent of the handle being activated. That means you just carried the ball into the end zone and got a touchdown. If things just swirl around and splash out of the bowl it might be time to consider professional help. Plumbers know things we don't and have seen things we would never want to, so if you cave and quake, it's going to cost you, but it's money well spent. It's not like calling a plumber is shameful or you're throwing your money down the toilet or anything. (Keep repeating this to yourself as you go for the phone.)

I was lucky, I didn't have to resort to dialing 911. I scored six points with no backsplash, which only comes from experience. Clean up was relatively easy involving running the new plunger under the bathtub faucet and then putting it away immediately behind the washing machine. "Out of sight, out of mind." My misery was over and I could exhale—until the next time.

The Water Nazi of Oakland

~~~~~~~~~~~~

Roommating is popular in California, where stories of staggering rent amaze newcomers and natives alike. This issue is second only to "Where are you from?" as many of the transplants compare notes.

Nobody asks the obvious, "What made you come to California?" This is a no-brainer. If you have to ask why someone moved here, you have no business being here yourself.

People move to California to get to the top of the heap—to see what life is like in the cool center of the universe. Reading about California is one thing, but California itself is something that must be experienced.

A close friend allowed me to roommate with her in Oakland and only charged me a token fee, which was extremely generous of her and unheard of in these parts. To this day I'm thankful from the bottom of my heart—and my wallet. My California education began there and focused equally on the legendary traffic jams, possibly the best (and most expensive) restaurants known to man, and a million other things, including and especially, the environment.

The Number One rule in any house where you become a roommate is to follow the rules of the landlord, right, wrong, or otherwise, without question or hesitation, unflinchingly, and ASAP. The feudal system is alive and well, and the new roommate is the true underdog here. Rules are posted, rules are obeyed, and the keeper of the keys reigns supreme.

It wasn't until years later I recognized any significant inequities here. Like a dog, I just pointed my nose and let the rest follow along, tail wagging. I always kept the door locked regardless of the side I was on, inside or out.

Several rules that were non-negotiable had to do with water use and container disposal. The recyclables were separated into glass, plastic, garbage, paper, light blue, dark blue.... it was endless. The little icon stamped in the bottom of plastic bottles was as popular reading as the label on wine bottles and was read with as much enthusiasm. It determined how the bottle should be categorized, sorted, and disposed of. But for me, it just led to immense confusion. More than once my roomie resigned herself to this duty in the name of expediency to make sure everything wound up in the proper bin. Heaven help us if some plastic snuck in with the glass.

Another set of rules, possibly even more important, was regarding water conservation, which completely blindsided me when I first moved in. Used to taking looong hot showers, it was easy for me to spend several days and nights in the bathroom singing, whistling, and practicing Karate. I thought nothing of ordering out for pizza so as not to be interrupted.

For those uneducated, the Bay Area is cool and damp 364 days of the year and the walls always remained ice cold. There is no appreciable amount of insulation in any of the walls and only a steamy hot shower would warm the bones.

The Water Nazi of Oakland

Running the furnace just didn't make sense. Everybody just added and removed clothing all day long.

This was when I discovered firsthand, by the way, how moisture condenses into clouds to form rain. The bathroom was miserably cold without any form of heat, except for a lit candle or two, and when I'd finally emerge from the hot shower, I found myself literally in a fog. I couldn't see my hand in front of my face and water droplets were falling from the ceiling, sort of making the bathroom into its own little ecosystem. It was like camping in the rain forest—indoors.

Ancient wisdom and modern common sense blend in the Bay Area, as Feng Shui sweeps through the land leaving balance and bankruptcy in its wake. Money arrives and departs on its own agenda as well, but California Feng Shui's innovative modifications and space age technology has apparently managed to arrest money's departure there, or at least slow it down as it were, through its control of the conventional toilet. The story goes like this:

Like penicillin, the *Feng Shui-McKenzie Correlation* was uncovered by accident somewhere around the turn of the century. It remains unclear where the credit lies, but we do know that a promising young plumber named John pulled a quilted pot-holder depicting a horse[1] from the jaws of an old fashioned toilet that possessed an almost supernatural quality of exuberant water pressure that is sorely missed today.

---

[1] The pot holder featured the common straight and the more engaging running stitch that was key in the evolution of knitting. "We didn't see the zigzag stitch until the Roaring 20's," appraisers commented.

81

The last I heard, the pot holder was on display in the Philadelphia Art Museum on loan from the *Plumbing Hall of Fame* in Camden, New Jersey. Blatant, arrogant cooing was observed when Baby McKenzie was confronted with the dripping pot holder, and he may as well have signed a written confession, solving the mystery. Blame was assigned to the toddler, and from then on the toilet lid, without fail, remained in the "down" position when not in use.

Shortly after this, the McKenzies came into an inheritance and became millionaires. Life was good. In fact life was great—until Dean McKenzie, the owner of the house, had a fight with his wife and left the lid to the toilet in the "up" position. It was October 29, 1929, which became known as *"Black Tuesday"* or The Great Depression.

As word got around, it was assumed that this little accident was the reason for the Great Depression and Dean never heard the end of it from his Feng Shui adherent wife, and needless to say, the writing on the wall was quite legible.

As a result, today an astounding eight out of ten households in Oakland practice the "lowered toilet lid practice." Thanks both to Feng Shui and modern water conservation, we can take control of our financial fate and enjoy the impact this has on our checkbooks.

The late John D. Rockefeller, Standard Oil tycoon, recommended we "...keep all our eggs in one basket—but watch that basket!" Feng Shui wisely teaches its followers to keep their crappers shut so their money will not exit through the bathroom plumbing and go down the toilet.

The Water Nazi of Oakland

Some friends of mine, entrepreneurs of sorts, did this and retired among the nouveau riche. They had 10 toilets installed and watched over them as a mother hen watches her chicks, making sure the lids were always closed. If one closed toilet lid saved money, imagine what ten closed toilets could accomplish. Money behaves differently in California, and apparently, so do the toilets.

But back to my Bay Area roommating—one more rule I should mention that we had to observe, and an appropriate way to bring things to an end, was the flushing rule. Although connected to a public sewer system, a special water rule was instituted via the *Preamble of the Water Conservation Act* of the house and posted in calligraphic script on the main wall of the bathroom: "If it's brown flush it down, if it's yellow, let it mellow." This was apparently a tried and true practice with septic tanks and is no doubt gospel in any trailer park. It was something abhorrent to me from my upbringing and it took great strength I barely knew I had, to comply. But once my landlady friend explained the reasoning to me, I was better able to cope.

Urine would sometimes ferment for a day or more while solids were immediately sent to the Grand Canyon (or wherever things went). This also logically meant that the window must remain open for ventilation purposes. The cool air, however, didn't know it was supposed to stay outside and made itself welcome inside, making the bathroom the most necessary but least inviting room in the house.

Although everyone has an innate ability to adapt to their environment, cold toilet seats will always remain a pain in the lower extremities. My bedroom was adjacent to the bathroom and I'd always subconsciously listen for the "yikes!" shortly after the door would quietly close. The seat got so cold it would actually stick to one, and your reflexes would kick in so you'd jump to your feet a moment or so after the "yikes!"

Often after standing up, the dang wooden toilet seat would hang on to one's underneath for a moment or two of horror before letting go, then it would slam down loudly to punctuate the howl of pain. This became such a novelty that soon everyone in the house was entertained by this nautical event and were trying to picture what was going on in there.

My landlady had explained the ecological ramifications of all this early in my residency, such that every time a toilet would flush anywhere in Oakland, someone over at the Hoover Dam, 569 miles south-southeast give or take, would have to open or close a valve to compensate for water use, barometric pressure changes, and wind direction, otherwise the shade of turquoise in the Aurora over the Great Lakes would flicker, and we couldn't have this. "We must think globally now," she admonished, and once we were all aware of this, we knew compliance was mandatory. We all obeyed without hesitation and only flushed when the unthinkable occurred and someone had a bowel movement.

On one occasion when company was over and one of them was relieving himself behind the closed bathroom door, we heard the tinkling of peeing and the immediate unmistakable sound of the toilet flushing, followed almost immediately by a loud through-the-door apology "EGADS! SORRY! SO SORRY! I FORGOT!" Nobody had heard the

"Yikes!" and the seat smacking the porcelain, so we already knew other rules had been broken and likely a hydraulics engineer at the Hoover Dam was spinning valve wheels at top speed and cursing under his breath.

One-Flush Willy

~~~~~~~~~~~

Immediately east of Los Angeles is the town of Ontario, California near Rancho Cucamonga. I was roommating there in an old 1895 Victorian mansion just off the Mt. Baldy exit. Today it sits on just barely an acre and sports about thirty trees, but at one time the old place was surrounded by three hundred acres of lemon trees.

The large gingerbread decked house featured the typical interior nooks and crannies of upscale neighborhood homes, along with ornate solid wood trim. The wide stairway and shiny wood banister, high ceilings and huge closets, and solid wood paneled doors, made it one of the finer examples of the Victorian Age. I considered myself lucky to find an affordable rental in such a historic area.

As the sole renter at the time, I had the upstairs bathroom all to myself; normally it would be a communal arrangement when the other rooms were rented. But before you could say "a bathroom is just a bathroom", trust me, some bathrooms are unique. And as bathrooms go, this one was head and shoulders above any I had ever encountered, before or since. In this bathroom was a modern invention created by the world's finest minds—a toilet unequaled by anything of its day—nor seen in commercial hotels for generations to come.

Bowlful of Laughs

When this house was built, people rarely spoke of 'technology' and simply labeled things 'new fangled contraptions'. Brooms, bottle openers, fly swatters, and firearms were all status symbols representing technology's cutting edge back then. And of course, at the top of the list was indoor plumbing. When the press was young and indoor plumbing was rare, talk of it was tantalizing and it was even considered newsworthy. Looking back, I wouldn't be surprised if the toilet upstairs was front page news in 1899, right up there with the Philippine-American War.

I must admit that at first glance I had my doubts about it—particularly when I saw the water tank mounted high on the wall and connected to the business end of the thing by a wide brass pipe. But once I tried it out, I was duly impressed with the speed and efficiency with which it took care of business.

On the front of this magnificent appliance was a carved ceramic bust that looked remarkably like Albert Einstein, but maybe with Mark Twain's hair. Or the reverse – it was a toss-up. No one could really decide who it was so we left it up to individual speculation or just free will. In fact, for a while we nicknamed him 'Free Willy'. Historians claim that he was destined to be delivered to Hartford, Connecticut to grace the Mark Twain Estate along with a graceful matching claw-footed bathtub, but the freight train made a wrong turn and he was delivered to California instead.

The wall tank featured a cute little pull-chain thingy with a teardrop-shaped ceramic handle that you'd reach up to grasp and give a yank to when flushing, but to be fair, you had to stand up to yank it. No one in their right mind could remain seated on this toilet without fear of losing something when the thing went off. Just the sound of its industry roaring to life was pretty frightening while still seated, but users quickly realized the need to stand up when they were done anyway or the enormous suction generated from the water evacuating would cause the dreaded "red ring syndrome" that could last up to a week in your nether regions and lead a medical observer to suspect the worst.

Those uncertain of its performance abilities—or theirs—were advised to 'pull and run' or ask for assistance, which is probably why the ceramic thingamajig was well out of reach of small folks in the first place. This heavy duty appliance was definitely rated adults only. In later years the manufacturer offered a donut-shaped safety adaptor for this model that fit around the rim of the bowl under the toilet seat and reduced the size of the bowl opening to circumvent the accidental loss of small children.

As time went by, my doubts about this toilet evaporated and were replaced by a healthy respect for this marvel of physics and hydraulics. Respect turned to trust, trust turned into friendship, and soon I affectionately dubbed my new friend "One Flush Willy". Before long, Willy and I confided in each other and exchanged treasures. There were certain times every day we were inseparable, or joined at the hip you could say.

Bumper stickers tout Los Angeles as the "Cool Center of the Universe." I always felt that if there were a center of the universe, and if Los Angeles was indeed it, then there had to be a "center of the center." After all, Los Angeles is a big place. So I wondered if this old-fashioned toilet might be the vortex of it all, a very portal to the other side. It was over a century old and had seen two world wars come and go, earthquakes galore, and yet it behaved as if it were brand spanking new. Now I knew why—One Flush Willy was the Center of the Universe.

It was apparent that the same minds that created the steamboat and the steam locomotive had a strong hand in Willy's design. With the way science continually moves forward, the designers apparently just brought their genius indoors and applied the same or similar mechanics to the creation of the indoor toilet. Experts at keeping things moving, these inventers didn't stop with human travelers, but extended their brilliance to keeping objects moving, no matter how unimportant or basic they seemed.

The graceful ceramic handle attached by a chain to activate this dynamic thing was obviously borrowed from the Mississippi Queen steamboat. I half expected I had awakened the whole neighborhood the first time I gave it a pull. The toilet's exuberance and fortitude were unmatched, as if the same limitless dynamics of Niagara Falls were at play here somehow. And while locomotives had no ignition system and relied totally on steam and pressure, theoretically they had no top speed. One Flush Willy gave the same impression as he seemed to have tapped into this same inexhaustible resource.

Soundproofing was in its infancy when this toilet rolled off the assembly line, so operational acoustics was an issue to be reckoned with. Since the jet engine had also not yet been invented, engineers relied on O'Brien's Decibel Rating Chart for comparison purposes and discovered that this particular model of "Clapper's Chain-Activated Hyper-Velocity Hydraulic Waste Removal Water Closet" fell somewhere in the vicinity of what was believed to be the mating call of a Tyrannosaurus-Rex and a backfiring 1932 putty-colored Dodge Pickup with a dual-carb slant-six and extended bed.

With Willy in a class by himself, certain things had to be considered. In California, windows are almost always open, so short of encasing the toilet in its own enclosure within the bathroom, there was no quieting him, and pulling the chain caused all the windows on the same floor to slam shut from the vibration alone. So strong was Willy's hydraulic suction that it dang near sucked the shower curtains down with each flush and slammed the door closed if it were open an inch. And I'm talking about the front door downstairs. More than once the seismic sensors in the San Andreas Fault were tripped when the chain was yanked, sending siren-blaring rescue teams speeding down the freeway.

Before the LA Freeway system, sound carried long distances, so a good portion of the neighborhood knew the status of everyone else's digestive tracts, day and night. If someone in the house had more than their fair share of roughage, everyone in Pasadena and Rancho Cucamonga knew about it. Nowadays noise pollution masks much of the racket so residents' internal privacy is better maintained.

I considered myself lucky that, although I shared the downstairs kitchen, I had the upstairs bathroom to myself.

In communal living, I've learned that the places where people "eat or excrete" can become problem areas and it is always a good idea to purposefully clean up after oneself. This is where Willy more than earned his keep. There were no holds barred with this baby.

One-Flush Willy

Willy had one purpose and one purpose only: the swift removal of any object or substance (no matter how vile) placed in the hopper, with whatever force was required (and then some). Nothing was left to chance. There was never any doubt. The sun rose, the sun set, and Willy flushed. All those nice things they say about the Golden State are true.

At the times it was necessary to improvise when cleaning up, Willy was always cooperative. He never wavered an instant when asked to dispose of leftover Brussels sprouts, halves of sandwiches, buoyant corks, cherry pits, melon rinds, an accidental T-bone, even a pair of underwear (don't ask), and was as dependable as a Swiss watch. Once yanked, I was confident the job would be completed in an efficient manner.

Not only did Willy swallow any food remaining after my meals, but he actually developed an insatiable appetite, until I felt obligated to feed him every so often. After swallowing hearty leftovers, he produced loud almost human sounds in the baritone range that could only be described as 'belch-like' or 'intestinal.' No one else in the house understood this phenomenon, so there were times his flatulence caused others to yell upstairs and inquire whether it was me or the plumbing making the obscene noises. Sometimes I got away with murder.

But unfortunately, even toilets with personalities are vulnerable to sickness. And one day, survivor of countless earthquakes, One Flush Willy fell victim to the common affliction that renders the strongest weak, constipation. And yes, I was guilt-ridden. It was at this time my roommate and landlord, Don, came to our aid. Lucky for us, he had a few tricks up his sleeve.

With a diminished appetite, and barely a shadow of his former self, Willy just played with his food. He was obviously fatigued and labored even when solids weren't involved. At one point as we tried to nurse him back to health, he came dangerously close to throwing up everything he had consumed over the last week, something no mortal should see. At least nothing my landlord should have seen.

"An old trick..." Don said thoughtfully with one raised eyebrow. He slowly poured a gallon of Clorox bleach into the feeble monster's gaping mouth with the skill of a surgeon's hand. It took a minute or two, but finally a dainty burp escaped Willy's large lips, followed a few minutes later by a second belch of monstrous proportions that shook the east end of Ontario. Don and I exchanged glances. It was time to pull the chain and step back—and witness the moment of truth.

Fortunately, the old boy came back to life with a vengeance, growling victoriously as he ingested the Clorox-jolted obstruction that had plagued him, having narrowly escaped the threat of surgery by the seat on his back. One Flush Willy had withstood the worst that humans could throw at him (I take no pride in this now) and once again stood tall—a toilet among toilets. This monument to man was still in the prime of life when I moved on to new adventures, having regained his rightful place at the bottom of the food chain.

The Flood of '88

~~~~~~~~~~

It was our first family trip to Disney World and although the following sunrise would find us screaming our way through death-defying rides, the thrills had already begun. The first was the plane ride, the first time the kids had flown, and then the rental van all shiny red, and finally the new state-of-the-art space-age toilet in the center of an oversized bathroom in our fancy hotel room in Orlando—a full-sized, clean as a whistle, commercial grade baby with a heavy-duty flush handle, inviting and fun for the whole family. Looming before us like a well-trained pit bull, this gleaming commode glowed beneath the recessed lighting with a spectacular spotlight aimed right on it.

Made in America with American pride, this toilet was in the prime of its life. It didn't have one battle scar; apparently it literally ate the enemy. With the strength of an ox —no, make that a water-buffalo—it clearly meant business and it wasn't calling in sick or going home early. If certain toilet models had names, this was obviously the "John Wayne." Although considering its location, perhaps a name like one of the park rides would have been appropriate, like White Water Mountain Log Flume.

When the flush lever was moved in any direction, this marvelous appliance sprang into action and wound up like a pitcher on the mound, starting with a slow spin that gathered both momentum and centrifugal force and then pitched its content out of sight like a fast ball. There's no doubt, this monster was leading the pack. If it had been a car in its previous life, it would have been a muscle car from the mid 70's—maybe an Olds 442.

As usual "Dad," (as I was called), always overlooked something. Overlooked? Dang, I was as blind as a bat. My kids picked up on it and knew instinctively this monster was dangerous. My youngest of the three, Alex, was only four and had recently hung up his diapers in favor of the more grown up way, but one look at this Modern Marvel and he was seriously reconsidering the tried and true, safe method of bathroom breaks that didn't involve all the loud noises, moving parts, and foaming water cascades.

Alex still had some issues with our home toilet. One was the claw from hell toilet phobia: the fear of something coming up out of the water and biting you in your vulnerables. Now, with a toilet seat so big you could drive a car through it, he suspected maybe newer and bigger menaces lurked outside the house. Combine this nightmare with an eight-gallon tank that could accommodate three electric eels and a Great White shark and the poor kid's imagination was running wild—he could only hope Mom had brought some backup diapers for the day in Disney World. Of course she did! She had to! Thank God for moms!

The Flood of '88

Alex's first experience with this new appliance brought him to a point of both shock and awe. He had used it and flushed it, then watched in silent horror as the whirlpool of death rose higher and higher toward him, then luckily, somehow knew to reverse direction, causing its contents to dive back down and disappear to wherever toilets take things. New Jersey, perhaps.

Although young, Alex was brave. And considering his unstoppable imagination, he was braver yet. Visions of being sucked down the pipe and swept out to sea raced through his innocent little mind. In spite of the air conditioning, and all that porcelain and steel, (not to mention the stone-cold temperature of the seat that proved an aggravation for all of us), after a mental struggle, he was able to temporarily set his fears aside. With the magic word "Disney" dancing in his head, he understood there were more important things on the table.

We all prepared for bed, too excited to sleep, but luckily sleep always seems to find you at times like these. We had worked hard for this vacation. We had saved. We ignored how long we'd had to wait for this trip. And we deserved this trip. Alex returned and hit the sack, and soon was asleep with George, his stuffed Basset Hound, tucked safely in his manly little arms.

Meanwhile, our 8-year-old twin girls were next into the bathroom, and suddenly through the door came bursts of laughter, shrieks of joy, and the pregnant pause that always followed, but then erupted again like Mount Vesuvius. Alex's older sisters always assessed new situations together and nearly everything was met with riotous laughter. Their laughter was truly musical to my wife and I, so out of sheer curiosity we'd have to investigate and see what was so funny. More often than not we'd join in, although we might not be laughing at what the girls found so funny, but more at the innocent and novel way they saw the world. The toilet flushed, the bathroom door swung open, and the two prettiest identical twins stepped out reeking of soap and toothpaste.

We settled in and the rest of us quickly drifted off. All was well until about 3 a.m. when Alex woke suddenly, having to go again. He had tossed and turned for awhile but came to the sobering truth that he must face facts or wet the bed. When he couldn't hold back any longer, he forced himself to crawl out of bed, stumbled hesitantly past the foot of our bed as we slept, and headed for the bathroom. He stopped as he spotted the nightlight we left on, which in this unfamiliar setting had taken on the glow of a fiery dragon in a cave. Hesitant but determined, he regained his courage and proceeded to enter the bathroom alone.

A few minutes after the door closed we heard the Anti-Gravity Shriek that every parent is familiar with. It builds a sort of reflex reaction that goes something like this: one of your offspring screams with staggering fear and the sound waves actually lift you out of bed and place you on your feet heading in the exact direction the sound came from—and only then do your eyes open. All this happens while the cry is still in progress. We had survived raising two colicky twins and Alex wasn't nearly the trouble they were, so responding to this reflex was like riding a bike. It probably follows you into the next world.

Bowlful of Laughs

In a split second both my wife and I were in the bath-room doorway to save him—and there we saw the Pit Bull toilet in Niagra mode, with wide-eyed little Alex, frozen in terror with nowhere to run. Only four years old with pajama pants around his ankles and a soaking wet bum, my panicked little man had backed as far away from the toilet as possible until his tiny rump was against the cold wall. That picture, seeing him tearfully fleeing the waterfall spewing forth from Big Bertha, haunts me to this day.

In most marriages, certain duties fall to specific parents. And plumbing problems, regardless of their size or nature, without fail fall upon the husband's shoulders. My wife dashed into the room, snatched Alex up, and flew out the door leaving me alone with the Grim Reaper of the Orlando Sewer System.

I understand the basic forces at work and how toilets function, but as the water level boldly climbed toward the rim without even slowing down, I too became scared beyond the capacity for rational thought and quickly contemplated abandoning ship. I was reminded of 'women and children first'... but then the rest of my family had instinctively bailed on me already. I thought it showed a lack of faith, but I stood a little taller and took a deep breath. This captain had no intentions of going down with the ship—or losing face before his toddler. With lightning speed I whipped every one of the billowy luxury towels within my reach off the bathroom towel bars and flung them on the wet floor to stem the tide of this turncoat toilet and fled—slamming the door behind me.

The Flood of '88

Rushing to the bedroom, I fumbled for the telephone and the number for Room Service. What had been the nicest hotel in the world with a sixth story view of softly waving palm trees suddenly began looking like an Everglades quagmire. With my neck hair bristling and goose bumps rising on my arms, I sensed something unearthly was afoot and rapidly punched "O", while my frightened little family huddled together on the bed behind me, their fearless leader, until help could arrive.

As I explained the urgency of our problem, Mom took everybody into the twins' bedroom so I could hear over their frightened whispers. I made my case and hung up, then I joined them and slowly we tried to regroup. I tried to see the humor in it but it was hard, because I was the guy who had forked over the credit card on the eve of our family's greatest vacation, only to have our lives thrown into a far-too-early morning upheaval. As always, the saving grace was the twins giggling unexplainably as we gathered waiting for reinforcements.

Before long an army of plumbers and hotel workers descended on us, armed with space-age pneumatic plungers and industrial-grade pipe wrenches. With waterproof jumpsuits, HAZMAT head gear, aspirator facemasks, goggles, and hip boots, the 6-man trained corp held a quick strategy meeting and the chief announced seriously, "Get ready, men, on the count of three we're going in! 1—2—3!" They thrust open the door to the inner sanctum and burst into the room.

101

We sensed a fearful confrontation as an unearthly blue glow from inside the bathroom filled the outer room and an ungodly voice answered their entrance with an echoing "I am TO-LER! Who violates The Throne Room?"

The second-in-command who had stayed with us held his arm out in front of us with hand facing backward in a protective way and said "Please stay back folks, and let us handle this," and we obediently backed further away.

The next thing we knew, with his small army backing him up, the chief advanced and dispensed some kind of blistering white ray from his unholstered weapon and the brilliant blue glow began to flicker. At last it faded and the menacing voice gurgled into the jaws of oblivion "I am To-lerrr......"

After a moment we heard the sound of a toilet flushing unremarkably, followed by a few calmly spoken words, and even a triumphant laugh. Then 'Florida's finest' filed out of the bathroom in triumph, smiling and patting each other on the back. Several waved or saluted in our direction on their way out as the hotel cleanup crew, buckets and mops in hand, filed in. I had lost my hero status, but the enemy had been beaten back and we had survived unscathed.

Cleanup was quick and uneventful and 30 minutes later we were somewhat calm again and all tucked in for the night, trying to pretend it was just a bad dream. Of course, Alex was firmly ensconced right between Mom and Dad, and the last thing I remember hearing was the girls in their own bedroom, still giggling incessantly, until I dropped off.

The next day, as we left for our first day of Disney excitement, we were apologized to by the staff and told we would be moved to a nicer suite when we returned. We had a great day on the rides, especially Space Mountain, but nothing compared to seeing the look on the face of the Italian-accented concierge when we later checked in with him to implement the transfer to our new room. The bellmen gathered around waiting for his instructions as he checked the register.

"You were put in Room 666?" he gulped in shock, "That's the room with the huge... no one was supposed to be assigned to that room since... Well! OK men, let's get their things out of there and into their lovely new suite! Zubbada! Zubbada!" as he clapped his hands in the air twice quickly for emphasis.

After the last of our things had been taken out by the bellmen and we had the kids in tow in the hallway, I couldn't help but hang back a bit as the nervous concierge closed the door tightly and stealthily whispered authoritatively into the ear of a small swarthy maintenance man. He grabbed up his tool bag and went right over and began installing a huge padlock on our old room.

We followed the men with our luggage to the other side of hotel on the same floor, where we were installed in a much larger suite with a very normal-looking bathroom and a gorgeous view, given vouchers for a free hotel brunch the next day, and spent the rest of the week enjoying Disney World as 'flood survivors'.

The Tiny Tot Toilet

~~~~~~~~~~~

One Madison Wisconsin summer when the kids were small, we accepted an invitation from some close friends and made plans for a one week get-away in Ocean City, New Jersey. We immediately began packing our things and those of our three kids, the 5-year-old twin girls and our year-old son, even though the trip wasn't scheduled until a month later. My thoughts drifted toward the inflatable zebra up in the attic and I wondered if it would still hold air.

Our friends were like most Wisconsin folk, true friends of the very best sort. We knew we'd have a fantastic time smearing ourselves with sunscreen, building sand castles with the kids, and enjoying fine dining afterwards. Babysitters were easy to find along the shore.

When July finally rolled around, my wife expertly directed the loading of our Subaru wagon inside and out; we looked like a one-car-parade coming down the road. The huge inflated zebra tied on the top of the car gave it a float-like appearance. With a vehicle full of vacation gear and kids, I had to remember to reach out the window periodically to make sure the thing didn't take off.

Speeds of 50 mph or more caused the zebra's neck to bend back and forth in the wind, giving it a life-like appearance of something struggling to escape its bondage on the roof racks. Possibly mistaking us for successful big game hunters or wildlife biologists bringing back a new species, sometimes cars in front of us even pulled over to let us pass. Unaware why, we simply drove on by, taking advantage of the road magically opening up before us.

The highway speeds would periodically cause the upside-down snout of the zebra to appear outside the top of the windshield behind the rearview mirror, and then obscure our view for about 5 seconds as it slid down the window to kiss the windshield wipers before snapping back upright. Vehicles all around us slowed as passengers laughed and pointed, even cop cars. But we weren't pulled over once. Truck drivers with heavy loads were especially empathetic.

As usual, traffic began to bottleneck the closer we got to Ocean City, which is actually on an island connected to the mainland by a causeway. From there it was a slow procession, but we maintained a prominent position by sporting the zebra, which isn't native to New Jersey. Part of the journey took us through the Pine Barrens where rumors of the Jersey Devil persisted, but no one in their right mind would get it confused with our zebra. Allegedly, it might have hooves, but it supposedly also had a menacing appearance, stood on its hind legs, and had a penchant for clawing car tires. The zebra just didn't fit the bill.

We arrived at the rental unit around Noon and began removing our things from the car and carting them into the first floor apartment. Bedrooms were assigned and everyone pitched in unloading. It's amazing how much work is involved in having a relaxing vacation! We toiled and sweated for a good hour or more before my wife and I sat down and cracked open some beers. The kids had immediately set off on explorations and every so often we'd hear an "Ohh" or an "Eewww" signifying new discoveries had been made.

Shortly afterward, our longtime friends, Roy and Erin, showed up with little Jack and Mathew in tow, beside themselves with excitement. Originally from the Midwest, they saw the Jersey Shore as an exotic resort. Arriving at the coast released some primordial emotions in all of us that were actively surfacing and everyone felt it. As we shared in the heightened emotion, nearly everything took on a positive note. The ocean does indeed have its romance.

Over the week we enjoyed miniature golf, swimming, body surfing, sand castle creation, seafood of every variety, both in restaurants and the rental units (theirs and ours), sunbathing, fishing, kite flying, late night TV, movies, all forms of shopping from souvenirs to food, walking on the beach, people-watching (how could you not?), and especially eating. Now was not the time to diet, now was the time to gorge, and gorge we did.

We feasted on every morsel available of crab, lobster, salad, sea bass, clams on the half shell, oysters, corn on the cob, Jersey tomatoes, French fries, pizza, cheese-steak hoagies, asparagus, seafood stew, wine, beer, iced tea—every gastronomic delight imaginable. Everything was available, so we were limited only by the size of our stomachs (which were growing daily).

There was one thing we hadn't counted on. Since Ocean City is situated on an island with no real water source, all the water is pumped in from the mainland and all the waste is pumped back there as well. Gravity has little to do with this process since everything is pumped sideways, not up or down. Engines of some sort must come into play to meet the hydro-needs of the island dwellers, and perhaps sometimes the machinery got tired. We began to suspect something like that when we noticed that even when the faucets were turned to *completely open*, all that came out was a trickle of rusty sludge.

The Tiny Tot Toilet

And being a vacation area, all functional systems were constantly pushed to their limits. It was immediately noticeable that the plumbing had its problems and nowhere was this more apparent than with waste removal. Veteran vacationers of the area, without fail, approached toilets with fear and trepidation while reciting silent prayers to the plumbing gods and crossing their fingers. The toilet plungers nearby were either well worn or brand new, neither of which boded well.

An old well-worn plunger meant it had fought in many battles. A shiny plunger meant there had likely been a recent system failure requiring the purchase of new equipment. So we had only one strategy: "We'll give it all we've got and hope for the best." Either way, it was a sort of Russian roulette and was probably going to be a 'multiple flush' event before things were over.

Unknown to many, every toilet has its own persona, and it's best to try to understand where they're coming from before dropping your drawers, sitting down, and opening fire. We often found it was best to send a child in first to 'prime the pump' so to speak, and then increase the pressure gradually so as not to overwhelm the toilet right off the bat. A little compassion goes a long way.

Our first evening, after finishing our non-stop daily feasting, we were seated around the table at our vacation place reminiscing, telling jokes, and recalling horror stories of sunburn, large fish, fish that got away, annoying neighbors, the whole gambit. Stomach rumblings became so common, everyone silently wondered who would be the first to bravely face off with the toilet. Nobody wanted to be the wet blanket and spoil things so we played a little waiting game that went on until the bravest (or weakest) soul stood up to excuse themself, which this time happened to be me. When you gotta go, you gotta go. Nature was calling me loud and clear, trumpets and all.

I entered the little room and looked around—the room had no window so it was pitch black. I pulled the light chain overhead and closed the door behind me. The bare 25-watt light bulb seemed to make the room darker as it flickered on. The toilet beckoned—dared me, in fact. I never saw such a small appliance. It had to be an antique—or a child's version. Did real people actually use such tiny bowls in centuries past? Or is it true that people today have grown so much larger than those of our past generations?

I approached it in slow motion so as not to scare it. I was hoping for the best, but prepared for the worst. The toilet creaked and even swayed a little under my weight. I consider myself somewhat of a normal size guy, but the toilet begged to differ and moaned, then began gurgling and complaining beneath me.

As luck had it, the toilet and I both pulled through, and the toilet curse that had plagued me most of my life seemed to have let this episode slip by unnoticed. I emerged victorious, and for all its minute size, I held this toilet in high regard for the week we shared these intimate moments. I even felt confident enough to read a bit while seated, assured that everything would work out at the end. I never asked the others about their private moments in there, but in future years perhaps any truths would come out.

Then all too soon our vacation was over. We sadly packed our things and were facing the long boring traffic jam that led to the mainland and home. It was worse because the entire vacation had gone perfectly. My wife, our kids, Roy, Erin, their boys, everybody had a memorable time we will never forget. No one commented on or complained about issues with anything, even the tiny toilet.

Bowlful of Laughs

Crestfallen, we saw ourselves slogging through the long year ahead before we could enjoy another vacation adventure together. Roy and Erin were facing airports after the monotonous drive, so they were especially sullen. We sadly hugged each other, Roy and Erin settled the boys in the car, and they drove off waving out the window.

Our car was packed too, but we had planned one last parade to the bathroom before departing. My wife and kids had uneventfully relieved themselves and freshened up in the bathroom and then finally appeared in the doorway and came out to hop in the car. But as soon as my son stepped out I noticed a quizzical expression on his face as he looked over his shoulder.

At first it was just a small dark cloud on the horizon, but then it gained momentum and turned into a veritable typhoon. In my complacency, it had struck—the *toilet curse* exploded on the scene with dizzying speed and caught me completely unaware. After all the punishment it had endured during the week, it was at this moment that the tiny little toilet had apparently breathed its last; a cloud of unmistakable death hung in the air.

It never fails, I thought—just when it's my turn. I poked my head into the bathroom and saw the miniature flush handle had snapped in two; the tiny toilet was done for—beat up from the feet up and officially 'out of order.' I visualized my wife inside comforting my little son before they came out saying "Now don't worry, just don't say anything and we'll let Daddy take care of it, okay, honey?"

The Tiny Tot Toilet

A hissing bubble emanated from inside the tank. I knew if I needed it, I would have to seek out an alternative option. I walked outside and closed the door, planning on walking into the brush behind the place or stopping at the first gas station we saw. But just then, I realized the apartment adjacent to ours was cleaned and abandoned, the former tenants already lost in the maze of traffic. A spark of curiosity ignited. I wondered what *their* place offered. The cleaning crew had left the door open and there weren't any signs saying Keep Out, so I walked over there with an air of anticipation.

Nearly identical to the place we had rented, the other unit offered little in the way of added convenience, and the appliances actually seemed a little older than in our rental; so much for exploration. But I only needed a better option than the woods—like a toilet that functioned! And suddenly I really needed to relieve myself. Last night's 'grand finale feast' had finally made it through my innards and was knocking at the door, so to speak. I had to go now. Why not here? Our place was closed, cleaned, locked.... *who's to know? 'a mailbox is a mailbox', right?*

I looked in the bathroom and there, amazingly, was *another* miniscule toilet, possibly even smaller, if that were possible, than the tiny toilet in our rental. The cheeks of one of my daughter's dolls might have overflowed its little seat it was so small. I instantly felt bad for the other renters, but there was no time for that. I had to decide, *Could I do this?* I knew I had no choice.

113

Bowlful of Laughs

Grand finales of one kind usually lead to grand finales of other sorts and my performance left nothing to the imagination. I was the bull fighter and the tiny toilet was the bull (or calf). Sometimes the bullfighter wins, sometimes the bull. This was my moment and I won, job done. I flushed the miniature handle on the tiny little tank and had a moment of shock and awe; nothing more than a benign little hiccup erupted from somewhere in the depths of the plumbing—a mocking hiccup, I might add.

Apparently the water was shut off to each apartment as it was vacated. Now I felt my face flush with embarrassment and I wasn't sure I would ever live this down. The 'flush' is intended as both a practical and a mental escape from facing what we carry around inside. Mine would now remain not only in my memory, but in full view of anyone who entered herein. I was mortified.

Unequivocally defeated, I buckled up and left behind what had to be considered *a bomb*. I felt bad. I felt remorse for the landlord, the next tenant, and surely, the plumber. Normally, the top of the tank is removed and placed across the seat as a warning—indicating an 'out of order' status, but in my shock I hadn't thought of that. I could only speculate as to the repercussions, the surprise, the disgust, the cleaner who might be fired, where the blame would be placed.... the *curse* had struck again!

Lost in Carolina

~~~~~~~~~~

Ahh! Vacation time! Our family was headed for the Outer Banks of North Carolina with a couple of relatives and the family of some close friends to really enjoy a week at the shore. We had a total of three cars in the caravan, with me driving one car and my 14-year-old son, map on his lap, riding shotgun. Our friends followed in their car with several of the younger kids, and four of the kids from both families who were old enough to drive brought up the rear in a third car with my wife as chaperone.

Since I knew the route best and had managed automobile-convoys before, it was my job to lead the procession. This later proved to be a big mistake, with the first bad omen appearing somewhere around the Chesapeake Bay. Chesapeake Bay Bridge is a bridge for most of its distance, but it also leads to a tunnel that submerges traffic under the bay, thus allowing ships passage through the Bay waters at strategic points.

Midway across is a restaurant, and facilities for fishing dot the bridge along its entire length. We were approaching the tolls on the Delmarva Peninsula at the south end of the bridge connecting Maryland's eastern shore to its western shore when we experienced the first "fly in the ointment".

I had had an eye exam very recently and my vision had checked out at better than 20/20, something I didn't even know was possible. The next thing I knew, I was suddenly having trouble reading the road signs. I never knew eyesight could fail that fast and a blind leader is never a good thing, so I was having to depend on my son's vision.

Of course, the people in the chase cars had no idea of the pandemonium that broke out in my car as my son grabbed the binoculars and began desperately shouting out the signs above and beside the road. Leaving nothing out, my son literally saved the day and I got a crash course in Maryland's littering laws and a blow-by-blow of how many miles it was and exactly where to turn to get to Bubba's Barbecue and Fred's Fireworks.

After some harrowing times experienced only in Car Number One, we arrived safely at Duck, North Carolina, our destination. When I was finally able to relax, I provided my son with snippets of history and geography lessons, explaining that we were not far from Kitty Hawk where Wilbur and Orville altered mankind's course forever in a positive direction (up). Thanks to my clever young co-pilot, I felt fortunate that our own trip had not altered it in a negative direction.

We arrived at our rental house, which was typical of the beach area and was built on pilings and stood a flight up off the dunes. We all reveled in our fast efficient arrival and set about unpacking, exploring, and talking about how great the week was going to be. The kids immediately became useless and began goofing off outside as the adults took on the organizing chores and assigned rooms. But even that took next to no time—we just threw everyone's luggage in the appropriate locations and started looking forward to a sumptuous shore lunch.

Activities began immediately as we speedily found a nearby all-you-can-eat 'in the rough' fish place within walking distance, and dove into some fresh seafood, fish and chips, French fries and drinks, plus ice cream sodas to-go for the kids with the bottomless appetites.

We came back and started right in playing board games while the kids immediately headed for the beach, smothering themselves in sun screen, building sand castles, flirting with the locals, and using their cameras to document every shell and grain of sand in sight. We had so much fun we got to bed late and our great vacation plans got a little sidetracked as we barely arose in time the following day to meet our planned schedule.

The morning found the teens pleading to be left alone for beach time (with those cute boys and girls they met the day before that they never told us about until later). So once the discussion was over (they won), my friend and I, our wives, and the two youngest children with us, were hurrying along at a quicker pace than we had anticipated.

With only half of the group, everyone squeezed in one car and we began navigating the only road in the area as we flew toward the ferry that would take us from Hatteras, then south to Cedar Island and the village of Ocracoke. My friend's wife suddenly voiced an urgent plea for a restroom, which hastened our pace. The kids laughed at everything, but the grownups were taking the restroom request quite seriously.

As long as I obeyed the speed limit and squinted real hard (no one seemed to notice and I confess, I didn't think to mention it to anyone), we were okay, and my eyesight, or lack of it, barely mattered. When we arrived, we drove aboard the ferry, emptied out of the car, and dashed for the rail to look at the water. My friend's wife immediately excused herself to go to the restroom.

My son had been reading some pamphlets he picked up at the restaurant and commented that this was near the spot where the Roanoke Colony disappeared in 1587 and became the *Lost Colony*. I began to idly wonder when the captain of *that* colony had last had his eyes checked.

We chatted and enjoyed the scenery for the time it took to get across, but I guess things must have a tendency to get lost in those parts because even once we were almost there, we realized we hadn't seen my friend's wife again after we boarded the ferry. We had no clue what happened to her until one of the kids had to use the onboard head and discovered a long line of impatient looking people snaking its way halfway around the vessel from forward to aft. Then we realized she must still be in there somewhere.

It wasn't until we landed and the last car was driving off the ferry (headed for the nearest bathroom, most likely), that we managed to enter the restroom en masse and pry the feeble, drained woman from the toilet and half carry her to the car. Perspiring feverishly and white as a ghost, she managed to gasp one word, "Imodium", which immediately answered some questions and posed new ones. We made her comfortable and I aimed the car toward town hoping to spot a drugstore.

Our collective I.Q. was leaning toward food poisoning, probably the shellfish, and possibly from a bad clam in the huge bucket of steamers we'd had the night before. Of course that was after we had discussed and dismissed the possibilities of malaria, black plague, gout, and poison ivy—yeah, the kids contributed some of those options and they were sure they'd discovered her problem, so now having a possible diagnosis, we moved on like a flash to speculate about a cure.

There was no hospital to be found (the highway was non-stop signage, but there were no big blue H's) and we wondered what a helicopter flight to the mainland would entail. For now, she just requested a restroom again and there was more than one sweaty forehead in the car as we anxiously panned left and right, with nothing but pine trees surrounding us.

At quarter mile intervals, vacant public parking lots appeared on the east—our left, as we drove south towards the quaint colonial town of Ocracoke. The parking lots were, no doubt, filled during the height of the summer season when shuttle buses would pilot endless loops transporting expectant sightseers and fidgety children to the historic little town.

Once there, the wise would learn what life was like before electricity when pirates commanded the high seas, while the *smaller and wiser yet* would drag their parents into souvenir and candy stores to shop and eat. Later, the buses would shuttle these same people, exhausted, sweaty, and whining, back to the parking lot where they could begin the search for their cars.

Out of the corner of an eye, someone noticed that these lots each sported a nice long row of portable *Johnny on the Spot* restrooms, lined up like brave soldiers facing a firing squad. Slumped over, head hanging, the sick woman's arm raised as if it had eyes of its own and silently pointed to the lot up ahead and the car magically sped into the next parking lot and steered itself to the row of sparkling blue and white fiberglass restrooms looking very like telephone booths without the glass.

She was clearly in emergency mode so at her insistence, we dropped her off and in a flash she disappeared inside. My friend and I exchanged glances and gunned it into town in search of Imodium [which I believe her husband now wears in an amulet around his neck].

The gastrointestinal gods were smiling and we found Imodium in Ye Olde Ocracoke General Store. We left my wife and the children behind there to explore and spend money, and my friend and I took off towards the north, laying rubber on the white cement pavement. We were on a valiant mission and the nearly deserted road was our race track.

A few seconds into this mission of mercy, as if on cue, my friend and I turned towards each other at the same instant and our jaws dropped. *Which parking lot did we leave her in? There had to be five or six parking lots along the high-*

way, each with their own set of 50 porta-potties, and they all looked alike!

Panic was about to set in when we pictured, in what we originally thought to be intelligent minds, a sick woman, mother of small children, stranded in a vast sea of parking lots with only a toilet seat for a life raft. What would the headlines read when a maintenance man discovered the body in the fall? Our minds raced as I pulled into the first parking lot and faced the row of toilets, wondering if my friend's wife was behind door number one or door number fifty. Blowing the horn didn't seem right, but what were we supposed to do? Knock on each door and call out "Honey, are you in *there*?"

We climbed out of the car to survey the landscape and just stood there, two idiots staring at a line of toilets, wondering what to do. My friend cupped his hands to his mouth and called out her name, not loud, but quite audibly. Not much happened. The sun went behind a cloud for an instant, that's all. We knew we were outsmarted and were consumed in thought when a police cruiser pulled up alongside us.

The sweat pouring down our brows probably made us look shifty-eyed and suspicious – how can you expect a cop to believe you lost your wife in a row of outdoor potties? His piercing glare was getting to my friend, who finally managed to stutter out an explanation. And before we finished, the cop figured out what was going on and instantly pursed his lips to hold back an avalanche of laughter.

For a minute our uniformed friend avoided eye contact, fearing this would open the floodgates to hysterics, first looking off to his left and then down at his feet. Then he closed his eyes and pinched the bridge of his nose and winced. Public servants everywhere share notes behind the scenes and this man knew he had a crowd pleaser handed to him on a silver platter.

Finally he raised his head, eyes red and watery, a mockingly serious expression on his face, and looked up, but as soon as our eyes connected the expression changed and he quickly had to look away again. It was clear he was ready to explode on the spot. Just when I thought for sure he'd blow a gasket, he held up the palm of his hand towards us as if to stop traffic, slowly backed away, got into the squad car, slammed the door, and *did* explode.

It's true that discretion is the better part of valor but even though he dropped his head down as if writing something, it was clear the big man had truly lost it. The entire squad car swayed as he emitted muffled hoots and hollers, then a sort of donkey laugh escaped into the air, followed by a partially stifled thirty-second hoot, and finally an exhaled roar as he began pounding on the steering wheel with both hands.

Unable to control himself any longer, he went right into a "wheezing, coughing, nose blowing" performance that could easily be heard above the vacation traffic, even with his windows up. We were nothing if not mortified.

With our backs to the bank of toilets, we hadn't noticed the wrung out, but clearly relieved woman dragging herself on her hands and knees across the ground from one of the potty booths to where we were. With one hand on her stomach and eyebrows raised, she reached up from behind us and startled her husband by putting her other hand on his arm and looked questioningly at the police car.

The trooper had lost any semblance of composure, but he managed to pull himself together a little when he saw my friend's bedraggled wife there with us. This pro-

123

vided his exit strategy. He quickly started up the cruiser and gave us a little wave to indicate he knew we didn't need his help, and dropped the car in gear. As he drove away, the need for restraint diminished with each yard of distance he put between us, and a new wave of laughter tore through him as, with tears in his eyes, he shook his head in disbelief. Finally I felt I understood the term "Always leave 'em laughing." This guy was clearly so useless now, that even if we had just robbed the local bank, we would have gotten a free pass on it.

The Innerworkings
of the Outer Banks

~~~~~~~~~~~

The Outer Banks of North Carolina has been a favored vacation spot for many and my family had their eyes on the area for our next one. If you look at the East Coast of the United States, you'll notice that North Carolina juts out into the ocean farther than any other state, placing it closer to the warm Gulf Stream where the wilds of the Atlantic thrive.

Numerous pirate folklore tales and even ghost stories are told about these waters, as well as yarns of many ship wrecks and skeletons of trading vessels still trapped in Davy Jones' Locker, lost to the plunderers that once plagued this area. It is said that Nags Head got its name from the schemes of land pirates who would hang lanterns on horses' necks so as they roamed the dunes grazing they appeared as lights on sailing ships to the vessels at sea. Those ships that changed course and followed after them, ran aground in the shallows and were boarded by pirates waiting ashore.

This rustic area, once Bluebeard's headquarters, is a magnet for surf fishermen and possibly the wildest and most desolate area along the entire East Coast, with the possible exception of the Maine shoreline. There are no lifeguards, few monitored beaches, and on a good day you can walk for miles without meeting more than one or two people. Some days you can just beach yourself and the surf, the sun, and the sand are all yours. The water is warm and fish can easily be seen even from the shore.

The bright sun, soft ocean breezes, and the relentless sound of the gentle surf combine to welcome you. Bonfires are usually permitted on the beaches and as evening comes on and stars begin to twinkle in the dark blue skies overhead, bright dancing firelights begin visibly dotting the shoreline. Total strangers unite in camaraderie around them. The rhythmic surf, soft laughter, and friendly conversation can just be heard above the background sounds of the crackling driftwood.

Rental units are relatively inexpensive and afford all the comforts of home including air conditioning. A string of towns with names such as Duck and Avon are situated on a thin island separated from the mainland by a wide shallow bay. On stilts, each vacation house has two flights up, with a kitchen, living room and bathroom on the first floor as you enter, effectively keeping most of the sand on the lower level. The upstairs living quarters are up a staircase to bedrooms at the top, all offering magnificent views of the mighty Atlantic Ocean.

The beautiful five-bedroom vacation home we rented had glorious views of the beach and surf to the east, and a meager civilization toward the mainland. Everything was laid out beautifully and the accommodations worked perfectly. It was only later that we became aware of a silent entity in the bowels of the rental that had waited patiently, menacingly, until we were all comfortably moved in, before striking.

My three kids, 16-year-old twin girls and 11-year-old son, were honored to each have their own room, as did my mom, who had temporarily made peace with my wife for the sake of the annual family vacation. Precarious as things were, the 'everyone-gets-their-own-room' strategy clearly seemed to be working. But while we excitedly made plans to visit Ocracoke Island, the Lost Colony, the lighthouse, the rustic beach, the quaint restaurants, and other attractions, unbeknownst to us, something evil was lurking downstairs making plans to take over our vacation and sabotage this oh-so-important peace treaty.

Fortunately, the next few days were marvelous and peaceful. And between excursions, the six of us dined out nightly on fresh fish, French fries, cole slaw, lobster, clams, oysters, scallops, and shrimp. We washed everything down with generous helpings of coke, beer, and wine which brought a little pizzazz to the occasion, specifically by speeding up our bloated digestive tracts. And then when it came time to relieve ourselves back at our rental home in the one toilet we had to ourselves, it clearly had its ceramic hands full as one of us dove in to the bathroom and the rest of us all lined up in the hallway near the closed door.

The first use was nothing spectacular. The little commode managed to get the job done but didn't truly impress its client. We weren't expecting glitz, just reliable functionality, but it did seem to already be working at capacity. And with every subsequent use-then-flush, the little appliance showed even less exuberance. By the third or fourth visitor, the toilet was clearly laboring to get its job done. Thus it came as no surprise the following late afternoon, when the toilet only fulfilled half its immediate obligations and I was soon on the phone to the rental office complaining.

Of all our adventures, dinner always seemed to be the best part of each day and usually the most fun. Thus we were hardly contemplating what was to follow hours afterwards as the digestion of each of us hit its peak. And lest you think that kids have less to contribute to putting the pressure on such a situation, think again. But as long as our personal plumbing was working well, we just assumed that the mechanical plumbing would be able to keep up with us. After our first call for repairs, we figured we were back to ground zero and at least on a 30-day warranty.

But just a day later, the toilet once again began showing signs of fatigue, so we then had another reason to get alarmed. In the midst of all that natural beauty and without a TV, the toilet was an obvious object of visual entertainment, so it didn't seem too anal to observe the whirlpool as it began laboring. It got started okay, and it flowed around and around okay, but when the time came for the unspeakable to disappear down that cavern that leads to regions unknown, it just gave up.

Moreover, the water/debris level was a little too close to the top of the bowl for comfort (where the worst threatened). An overflow condition could only be met with screams from the current embarrassed user and beating a hasty retreat. So once again, after yet another family member fled the bathroom in panic, and this time with exasperation in my voice, I demanded help from the rental office.

This time the 'super' himself answered the phone and after a short conversation promised speedy help. He showed up a short time later in an ancient little dune buggy/golf cart that, although it was fast, it was clearly on its last legs— or wheels. One headlight was knocked out, it had a crumpled rear end, and multiple dents, dings, and scrapes. And to add to our concerns, before we had a chance to experience the relief that help had arrived, we realized that our hero plumber, dressed in very casual garb right down to his bare feet, was not only less than organized, but quite drunk as a skunk.

We gathered in the downstairs doorway to watch the beginnings of this rescue operation as our superhero parked on the top of a nearby sand dune and stood up unsteadily in the front seat to lean into the junk-filled rear of the vehicle and dig through his gear for what we guessed was a toilet plunger.

Staggering precariously into the house through a flock a circling seagulls that he seemed to have brought with him, he greeted us happily with a loud slurred "Hi there, howyadoin?" and without waiting for an answer proceeded directly to the bathroom. He removed the back of the toilet tank and dove right into his job, clinking, clanking, plunging, and flushing, for a good fifteen minutes.

L. Webb

Ultimately, he declared victory and said the toilet was safe to use, spared us a handshake, hopped in his rod, and vanished down the road (with seagulls in pursuit) at rocket speed, partially airborne as he weaved from side to side on the narrow beach road. Once alone, we gingerly flushed the toilet for a test run, and sure enough, it worked fine. Our troubles were over... we exhaled.

The next few days we continued to relax and tour the local area. We took the ferry to Okracoke island, worked on our tans, and inevitably found ourselves at the roadside fresh fish stand each evening where the delicious shrimp and assorted fresh seafood delights were procured for yet another fantastic dinner... not a care in the world.

Did I say not a care in the world? That was until the line formed again that night for our single bathroom that was acting the slightest bit annoyed about not getting its own vacation. This Friday night the very first flush proved fatal as the toilet died with a full load. A call to the golf cart repairman proved futile–as he was on break and it was impossible to determine when help would arrive.

At the same time, five more digestive tracts were actively processing one of the largest dinners we had consumed to date. All our bowels were sending emergency messages to our brains. With crossed legs, several phone calls ensued and we were told we could 'use the rest room at the main office', which immediately resulted in an angry explosion from both my wife and my mom. They actually agreed on something! They felt that by paying rent we were entitled to our own private bathroom. Trouble was brewing.

Various forms of rationalization were rapidly taking place and several people, I won't mention any names, felt justified in using the commode anyway, whether its unseen parts worked or not. The toilet seat worked and that seemed adequate, as processed shrimp, clams, fries, spaghetti, blue fish, oysters, beer, wine, asparagus, and salad exited and made their way into the plumbing of the temperamental toilet. Not one, or two, but three people shared this rationale, and sorrow was already mounting for the poor *plowed plumber* who was about to enter hell, drunk or not.

When the golf cart finally showed up, it was bringing a team comprised of the 'super' with a young apprentice, along for his trial by fire. The helper took one look at the 'job' and promptly became violently ill. I'm sure he finally found his calling in another trade, maybe landscaping, painting, electronics, who knows?

But the golf-cart plumber stayed, almost sober this time, and actually located the reason for the recurring problem. It turned out to be a mere pin hole in the ball float that permitted the toilet to function properly only once—until it gradually, slowly, filled up with water and sank gracefully to the bottom of the tank, allowing the water to escape in slow motion, bubble by bubble. It might take overnight, but it was no good under stress! And with more than one flush in ten minutes, the tank was still empty and the next flush was doomed to bomb. Well gosh—all we had ever needed would have been a big bucket of water! This was a new one on all of us.

It wasn't an easy diagnosis, but this guy had obviously been down in the trenches before and he knew his stuff. He took it in stride, plunged the debris, and replaced the float. Now we knew why he drank. The alcohol in his breath was strong enough to disinfect and fumigate his surroundings; a decided advantage in his line of work. And despite his working conditions, he was always fairly cheery and pleasant— you had to give him that.

The last few days of our vacation went off without a hitch, and a valuable lesson was learned for our future getaways. Whenever checking out a vacation rental unit, we ignored the niceties, the view, the soft beds and carpets, and headed straight to the bathroom and flushed the toilet at least three times. Evil lurks in places we don't normally expect and it's up to us, the savvy vacationer, to root out these demons wherever we find them. Toilets command all the power—and can make or break a pleasant vacation stay.

L. Webb

Hey, You Got the Time?

~~~~~~~~~~~

In a busy auto dealership, where the sales showroom and crowded service garage were linked only by a ramping hallway off of which was a tiny all-too-public one-person bathroom, employees and customers alike who needed such an accommodation were sometimes forced to leave the premises in search of facilities at truly inopportune times.

Inconvenience when the room was occupied, delaying either a sale or a customer payment, was bad enough, but at the worst of times, the frequently overflowing toilet provoked everyone's frustration. In the business world, the magic of a hearty handshake all but disappears as nature, declaring an escape from a tight place, suddenly claims everyone's attention from the next room.

So when the dealership drafted plans to expand, they did so unexplainably without moving any of the existing outside walls. This actually meant rearranging the interior and resulted in less room instead of more. New window offices, interior cubicles, privacy walls, and the same little bathroom were now crammed tightly into the already too small service shop. Employees were working almost in each other's laps.

Bowlful of Laughs

The arena of commerce and the science of waste elimination were separated by a pathetically thin wall incapable of concealing acoustics, and there was yet another design flaw. The little bathroom was supposedly-cleverly inserted into the busiest part of the building for convenience, with a commercial sized, big-boy toilet designed to accommodate the largest ass in the company–which it probably did.

When seated, one's left knee was inches away from an outside wall made of those clear wavy glass square blocks that were supposed to shield the user from the prying eyes of the curious. The right knee was just as close to the door. Just one thin wall away, on either side, was where people did business, dropping off and picking up cars, smiling, complimenting, berating, screaming, pounding fists, and shaking hands; and sometimes just standing around waiting for a car to be fixed.

Between the loud conversation heard clearly through the door from inside, users and the department outside ended up frequently being privy to each other's most private moments. More than once flatulent noises interrupted price negotiations at the exact moment when a credit card was being handed over by the customer and the service writer tried to yell a 'thank you' over it.

Inside the room, with the sun streaming in through the glass blocks on sunny days, a simple bowel movement felt like the stage curtain rising on one's 15 minutes of fame, with spotlights and all. When a potential customer excused themselves to use the facilities, employees toughed it out to keep their jobs and told jokes loud and long to provide a privacy cover until the possible 'sale' returned to the table. But some customers who experienced this intimate location, and often felt trapped inside too embarrassed to disembark, never returned to finalize a sale. Those of us who worked there knew the sagest of advice was never to 'get down to business' in that little room on a busy day.

On one particularly rough week, repairs were getting done late, so payments were also late and sales were being delayed until Friday. To add insult to injury, the toilet began overflowing and spilling its guts onto the floor, which promptly flowed out under the door and into the service area, making things both untidy and a tad slippery as well. And for once things rolled appropriately uphill; employees notified management, management notified upper management, and upper management notified the boss, who immediately called the plumber and demanded prompt attention.

The plumber showed up later the same day, driving what appeared to be a hardware store on wheels, gathered his toolboxes, weaponry, and SCUBA gear, and solemnly entered the arena.

After an hour of plunging and untold lengths of gunk-coated snake, he returned to the main corridor with head hanging. He had been unable to resolve the problem. In a fix-it environment such as a car shop, everyone understands 'intermittent problems' that never reveal themselves to the one paid to correct them; they frustrate the best of mechanics. And true to form, the toilet was suddenly on its best behavior, so the plumber had to dig deeper. After abandoning the preliminary diagnostic strategies that produced no results, he donned swim fins, goggles, and snorkel, tied a nylon rope to his left ankle, and flipped backward into the bowl.

A spotter awaited his return, but seconds turned into minutes, and minutes turned to hours. Shortly after the two-hour mark, when a crowd had gathered like polar bears around a seal hole, up popped a triumphant hand holding a gold Timex watch. Soon the plumber himself emerged beneath it from the depths of the bowl. And yes, it had kept on ticking.

The plumber speculated the metal-flex band was the most likely cause of this calamity. It probably twisted, stretched, expanded and contracted, and did all those things toilets and plumbing were not designed to compensate for. The watch's owner, no doubt too embarrassed to speak, remained silent and was likely late for all his future appointments.

In spite of this heroic effort, pinpointing the object of this enigmatic problem only seemed to reignite the boss's frustration. A reward was immediately offered for information leading to the capture and punishment of the perpetrator. A quick glance around the room revealed a watch on everyone's wrist. While unlikely, under breath murmuring was quick to suggest a customer might be responsible, anything to shift blame and get the boss's beady little eyes off the crew.

We all lined up and stood at attention as our short, stocky little boss walked back and forth in front of us, seething. Nobody moved a muscle. He spoke slowly and dis-

tinctly and we learned of the utter depravity of a person who would drop something into a toilet and not have the fortitude, *the backbone*, to speak up! We heard what wrath would fall upon this individual once he was ratted out, and we shuddered and hoped it was no one we knew. The boss ordered the watch sterilized in antifreeze, to remain on the front desk in a plastic bag as a reminder, waiting for someone to claim it—and to simultaneously convict themselves.

The ranting went on for many minutes, until the boss actually became so choked up with anger, he couldn't speak. He simply held up his hands, signifying the lecture was over and we all silently slunk away, each fondling his or her own watch as reassurance. I believe *only I* noticed when he put up his hands, that the boss himself wore no watch. In the interest of workplace safety, my lips remained sealed.

A week later, the same toilet came down with yet another ailment. After the flush, the sound of running water was heard well beyond the point silence should have stepped in. No one wanted the information to leak upstairs and have us risk the boss's wrath again, so one industrious employee volunteered to take a peek. Some of us gathered around and watched as he gingerly approached the toilet. Just as he was lifting the top of the tank off, a voice behind me yelled "Hey, if you find a watch in there, it's mine!" The crowd roared—and then we instantly made ourselves scarce.

Get Behind Me, Tonto!

~~~~~~~~~~~

Another auto dealership where I worked had its own version of expansion problems. It was an appropriately tight-knit little community. The hierarchy within boasted a variety of rewards and punishments based on one's seniority, productivity, and the usual unfairness of whether the boss liked you or not. The external hierarchy was defined by your membership in one of the three pillars of the dealership: *Parts, Service, or Sales.*

Sales brought in the dough, so salesmen were at the top of the food chain. Service, in second place, fought fires and kept everything humming along, and Parts was a necessity that just needed a bunch of gophers and one good man for a fearless leader—and that was me.

The owners had recently decided that the fastest way to increase sales would be to expand the auto showroom area to more customers by transitioning from four cars to twelve cars and glitz up the general showroom sales environment with office privacy panels. A new second floor built over it would house management offices with a mezzanine that looked out onto the showroom with a staircase directly down to the sales floor.

To the employees, this was almost as exciting as putting a man on the moon. It seemed we would soon be on

141

the map and we all suddenly held our heads a little higher. The salesmen had more cut in their strut and the office assistants had a new glide in their stride. We were movin' on up!

Located between Philadelphia and New York, employees and customers alike included both some backwoods hillbilly rednecks and some cosmopolitan city dwellers. Everyone was unique—just like everyone else. Some of our big guns included Rich, the Shop Foreman and possibly the best wrench turner the world has ever seen, and Fred, Head of Sales, whose expertise on where to place the decimal point had made him a legend in his own time.

Fred grew up in New York City, which immediately set him apart. He understood a side of life that was unknown to most people, such as building construction from the ground up. Like everything, the various segments of construction have their idiosyncrasies as well as their demons to contend with and no one knew that better than Fred. One of the main operations to be vanquished was proper installation of the *Gwavia Tuoilo*, the common toilet. As with many great discoveries, it was quite by accident that we in the lower echelons of the enterprise learned of an imminent danger associated specifically with that instrument.

After years of us all sharing an antiquated pair of rest rooms downstairs that met the barest requirements for space, cleanliness, and privacy, the new construction had brought with it the unexpected reward of including a new state-of-the-art restroom facility on the new second floor. We were all delirious at the prospect—but we had barely begun celebrating the completion of the plumbing, when we heard that the new bathroom was already in jeopardy.

The physical location was directly over the sales offices in the downstairs showroom and it had just been discovered that flushing the toilet resulted in nearly immediate indoor rainfall right through the showroom ceiling. And not just anywhere, but right on Fred's everyday work life as the chief car salesman whose sales desk was located just below.

We were all privy to that *"Voila!"* moment as we watched the owner enter the showroom, stare at the ceiling above Fred's desk, and yell "Go ahead!" As if by magic, there was the sound of the toilet flushing upstairs, followed in roughly sixty-five seconds by water droplets appearing on the ceiling out of nowhere and gracefully proceeding along the downward angle of the ceiling to the lowest point and beginning a steady drip. If Fred were seated at his desk, the drizzle seemed to zero in on the top of his head, centrally between his ears and midway between his flawless hairline and the back of his neck. Point taken—a pigeon couldn't have had better aim.

Beginning students of Hydroponics 101 are quickly introduced to the concept that gravity draws liquid to its lowest point, which under most circumstances is a direction we refer to as *down*. None of this mattered to Fred, of course, who was on the receiving end of the drizzle. And while it wasn't rocket science, at least temporarily the boss was allied with Fred that this had to be addressed immediately.

The experiment seemed to prove that the flush was inevitably followed by the drizzle, but once news of these investigative exercises made the rounds, the rank and file quickly got involved and silently began forming a line upstairs by the bathroom door. As the traffic increased, it appeared uncannily as if the opposite were taking place and the flush followed the rainfall.

Then the boss became ambivalent, so Fred had to tap his creativity and devise a more insistent stance to at least cause the bathroom closure, even if it meant having it condemned and sealed off from both public and private use. A large CLOSED sign was taped to the door, the plumber was called, and everyone went back to work.

About an hour later, Fred again found himself under a drizzle, and then a downpour. And on investigating, he discovered that the CLOSED sign had mysteriously found its way into the trash bin, probably because from a user standpoint, everything seemed to be functioning fine. The line had formed again and the entire group appeared enthusiastic, from the elimination process right through the water recovery process that prepared the shiny new toilet for its next flush.

Fortunately for Fred, help arrived shortly. The plumber assessed the scene and attempted a diagnosis— but it was later in the day and by then the crowd had gone home and the drizzle had dwindled to nothing. And that was the scenario for the next week: drizzle is drizzling, plumber comes, ceiling is dry, but Fred is wet and mad; plumber leaves, drizzle returns, Fred gets wetter and madder.

Everyone's crystal ball seemed to be a little out of whack, but even those who disavowed any dealings with ESP could plainly see the drainage issues Fred faced, as literally as if he were being targeted by an air-to-surface missile. He was frustrated, hurt, and disgusted. It took everything the plumber had to keep a straight face when Fred, 'Mr. Serious Face', pointed concernedly up at the ceiling with eyes enlarged by his coke bottle glasses, his thick dark eyebrows pursed and his bushy black mustache twitching, giving him more than a passing resemblance to Groucho Marx.

Whether it's TVs, Toyotas, or trampolines, intermittent technical problems plague servicemen everywhere. *"If it ain't broke, ya can't fix it."* But these words just fuel rage once the problem has been found, fixed and paid for, and then, suddenly… it's *baaaack*. As if the devil himself threw a switch, the ceiling that never leaked for the plumber began drizzling happily the moment his truck disappeared over the horizon, followed by Fred's whiny *"Oh fer cryin' outloud!"* exclamation and everyone else's muffled hysterical laughter.

New Yorkers don't become cynics overnight, but one was forming in our midst. As days turned into weeks, Fred began finding little gifts from co-workers to comfort him, mostly gaudy circus clown umbrellas unobtrusively tucked beside his desk. Up and down the seesaw bounced—fixed, not fixed, fixed, not fixed… Finally someone took pity on Fred and pointed him toward "The final word in toilet repair," *John's Johns*.

The following day, the unrepentant poltergeist that had invaded and possessed the upstairs plumbing was facing its final eviction notice. John, the master himself, arrived and toured the premises, armed with what appeared to be an amazing three-and-half-foot heavy-duty commercial-head toilet plunger in his tool belt, a twenty-pound positive-torque Stilson wrench in his left hand, a stethoscope around his neck, and what many later reported as a three-inch thick corned beef on pumpernickel with mayo and mustard in his toolbox.

A man in his prime, John was medium height and medium build with perfect sideburns and mustache, and bore a striking resemblance to Clark Gable. His eyes had a reassuring gleam of intelligence and his confident demeanor suggested he had served Uncle Sam and done him proud. A prominent facial scar like that of an upside down question mark proudly etched his left cheek where no attempt to hide it could conceal this mark of bravado.

He carried not one, but two snakes, as they're called in the industry; each coiled and worn diagonally from left shoulder to right hip and right shoulder to left hip. He was the very image of a classic Mexican bandito decked out in bandoleros full of ammo shining in the hot desert sun. There was no question in anyone's mind—he was a man among men. We all began picking up a strong sense of inspiration as our small group followed him as one, but at a respectful distance.

But then as the rank and file heard yet another plumber was to try to assess the problem that might threaten their toilet privileges, the crowd grew from three casual observers to a 1970's protest group, ten strong and rather imposing, and then somewhere along the line began to transform into the typical 'angry crowd of peasants with torches' like those in the movie *Frankenstein*. We needed that bathroom!

146

Get Behind Me, Tonto!

The mob followed John upstairs as an electric anticipation filled the air and subdued the crowd. John never turned once or even acknowledged what had the makings of an unruly mob, but he knew they were there. This was not the first time he had been in such a situation, nor would it be the last. John solemnly approached the bathroom with the respect a hunter shows as he approaches his fallen prey, knowing its fate is in his hands, yet cautious lest it might rise up in an unexpected final bid for life to leap upon him.

Hearts raced as John stopped, the bathroom doorknob hidden in his left hand. His other hand, raised behind him with fingers straight and his palm toward us, stopped us in our tracks and instantly hushed any sound the crowd even thought about making. His index finger then assumed the *"One moment..."* position. A solitary bead of sweat in the center of his forehead threatened to run straight down his nose, but undisturbed, he pushed on the door and went in alone.

Normal sounds of spigots turning and water running made their way through the door as everyone came out of their hypnotic trance. The crowd began to glance at one another nervously and started to back away, uncomfortably feeling like peeping toms. Throats were cleared and everyone suddenly realized *they* didn't want to be the last one standing there when John came out. The group broke up and hesitantly dispersed.

An hour later, Rich, Fred, the Service Manager, and myself were holding an impromptu meeting in the ramped hallway that connected the showroom with the Repair Department. Deeply involved in a business discussion, we were taken by surprise as a deafening silence instantly

147

smothered all workplace conversation. John, plumber among plumbers, had appeared at the top of the stairs, snakes coiled, and mission accomplished. It was almost reminiscent of St. Peter's Square.

With formalities out of the way and the hushed crowd gathering about him again, John came halfway down the stairs to address the crowd and launched rather eloquently into his now-famous and long-remembered speech that connected the course of human events with simple physics and sewage hydraulics, touching on parts of toilets we had never heard of before linked to procedures and operations that sounded downright death-defying and mind-boggling.

As car guys, we always secretly enjoyed tossing out the names of unknown tools and parts to our customers just to see their puzzlement and gain their admiration. But now it was our turn to say "huh?" We were all totally left in the dust—even Fred. Until, that is, his speech ended with two words with which we were all familiar—'ballpoint pen'.

At this point John produced the innocent-looking perpetrator that had been trapped in the evacuation pipe, accumulating a beaver dam of wet toilet paper and who-knows-what-else as it aggravated the already overtaxed waste separation chamber, and probably did the Macarena for all anyone knew. His silver tongue hypnotized us and left us in a state of stunned silence.

Finally, once again, he reassured the anxious crowd in a calm voice that 'this has happened before and could likely happen again', but that he was 'no flash in the pan'; he had handled many such emergencies and stood ready to defend us from all future catastrophes.

148

Get Behind Me, Tonto!

149

John continued slowly down the stairs and through the crowd, beneficently making warm eye contact with each of us. He deftly placed the pen in the mesmerized shop owner's hand, almost saluted back at us, and vanished out the front door. Nobody knew whether to shout, clap, or break into the song, when we heard someone speaking in that low, awe-struck tone reserved for the aftermath of a Lone Ranger episode when the sheriff has just asked "Who was that masked man?" Rich must have read our minds when he said "I don't know who that guy is, but he sure knows his sh_t."

The Last Poker Game

~~~~~~~~~~

The large Used Car lot and Auto Body Shop had many new additions over the years, the last one including plans for an employee lounge that never made it into the final design and left plumbing where there was no need for any.

The new addition on the drawing board again promised this space, this time for a locker room. The plan would utilize the plumbing for shower stalls and toilets, and include a lounge area with chairs and tables. Within a few short months, employees had the closest thing they'd ever had to a Rec Room—with everything you could ask for, except ample lighting.

The dark cavernous room surrounded in cinder block with a men's room environment on one side, and lockers and vending machines on the other, soon became a favorite hang out during breaks, when waiting for customers to claim their cars, and after work just to relax with the guys.

And the sheer beauty of it was, it was the last place that Mr. Burns, the boss with his own executive washroom, would ever show up in a million years. So it slowly became the place we clandestinely began hosting various forms of gambling entertainment that removed money from some pockets so it found its way into other pockets at dizzying

151

speed. Eventually, the bathroom in the back of the shop was where we set up our *never-ending poker game*. This became the highlight of many long days when the clock stood still.

What started out as a friendly game of Canasta one fine day in May, grew into quite an operation, soon involving the entire Garage and Parts Department. And since *green money* was the only requirement for membership, and the most important one to keep things going, we began working on recruiting the salesmen as well.

Novice players had to yield and learn as they played. One reason for that was new and younger recruits often had trouble remembering which type of hand beat which, so it became an annoyance met with sarcastic comments and raised voices if one of the veterans had to repeat himself. The more often the same question was asked, the more annoying this became, so one of the House Rules was that 'The discussion of hands and how they rank is strictly forbidden while the game is in progress.' After all, this could upset the players' composure and possibly give away someone's hand.

Once Mr. Burns left for the day, the word went out and the crowd would grow. Very quickly the poker game became a respectable spectator sport with people lining the walls and talking in whispers as fate would unfold before their eager eyes. The ante was only a dollar, but that didn't stop watches and car titles from being exchanged, mortgage payments being missed, and many questions being raised back home over the kitchen table.

We had an elaborate, if not sophisticated, security system in place that warned the players of Mr. Burns' approach. Should he show up unexpectedly, any mechanic in the shop with an air wrench in his hand when he saw the boss, even far off, would promptly issue three short even blasts in close succession: *Bthththt! Bthththt! Bthththt!*

If anyone outside the room was near the bathroom door when the boss appeared out of nowhere, the unmistakable knock on the door, *shave and a haircut-two bits*, was employed.

In December, when work in the shop had slowed to a crawl, we had one of our larger games cooking and tensions were running high. After the final card was dealt and the betting began, it looked rather obvious that all four hands were contenders, or else we had some mighty good bluffers. (Maybe both, it's hard to tell in poker.) There had to be forty dollars on the large round table.

There was standing room only and excitement was in the air. The place was packed and it made the crowded room suddenly seem small. Sweat broke out on Sonny's forehead and a pulsing vein above his eyebrow we had never noticed seemed to sprout up out of nowhere. It was easy to see what was going on in his head—there was a distant panic in his eye.

Sonny had a good hand all right, maybe a straight or a flush, but he had forgotten the rank and wasn't sure how good his hand really was. Whatever it was, by the way his eyes darted about and then riveted on his cards, three things were certain: one, Sonny was a lousy bluff; two, he had a good hand; and three, he didn't know how good. The pressure was on.

Bowlful of Laughs

It was just at this moment Big John came rushing into the men's room on a mission with a look of great concern on his face. John was in a hurry and everyone knew better than to stand between a fullback and his toilet, so the crowd cleared a path instantly—a wide path.

Oblivious to the invisible but overwhelming electricity in the air, John hit the middle stall and demonstrated what only he could do. He obviously found the collective moans and groans humorous as he set out to accomplish what he had come in there for. Gambling was of no interest to John and the thought that he might be raining on some local parade never concerned him for an instant.

The gamblers knew they were simply in the wrong place at the wrong time. As the atmosphere thickened, only the biggest pot in the game's history could have held the crowd there. But the biggest pot in the new bathroom's history was about to have the opposite effect - there was fire in the hole!

John flushed and the sound of his belt buckle on the floor absently told the crowd he was getting ready to make his exit in another few minutes. No one noticed that the flush sounded oddly muffled. A second later John's "Wo!" claimed everyone's attention as the door burst open and he stumbled out of the stall looking backward, still pulling his clothes together, and followed by a steadily increasing wave of brown lava on the floor.

Things began to happen fast. The crowd's survival instinct kicked in and, game or no game, it was overwhelmingly obvious it was time to go. In fact, it was *every man for himself* and the mob was virtually in stampede mode when the unmistakable sound of knuckles on the door drummed out *shave and haircut-two bits*, not once, but twice, indicating a raid was imminent. Some may have missed the message as it was already being drowned out by the sound of running feet.

No one could get out of the bathroom fast enough. Everyone tripped over everyone else and all that could be seen was butts and elbows as various groups in the panicking herd beat their own paths and spread out in different directions as soon as the threshold cleared. For a moment the doorway was clogged with a wave of humanity, a literal tsunami of sweaty men, who pushed clear of the clog and then another wave bigger than the first, spilled out into the shop, stopping the approaching Mr. Burns in his tracks.

The panic was such that no one realized who was in their way and the anonymous Mr. Burns was momentarily lifted by the crowd and carried backwards several yards before being dumped to the side on the floor where he then became just a hurdle to be cleared as the men leaped high into the air to continue their escape.

With the boss on his hiney back against the wall and 26 pairs of feet barely missing his head as the crowd rumbled madly over him like a bison stampede, the boss covered his head with his arms and wondered why he hadn't heard the fire alarm go off. Barely a few seconds later the place was silent, emptied to the last man and no one left in sight. Mr. Burns dizzily got to his feet, tried to dust himself off, and waited to smell the smoke. Nothing.

His curiosity getting the better of him, Burns pushed open the bathroom door and walked in, where he was met by the noxious odor and the deadly aftermath of the eruption. He stood in the middle of the room looking at the tell-tale table covered with cards and crinkled bills surrounded by overturned chairs on the floor all about it, where table legs and all, and now his own shoes, were engulfed in an inch of chocolate pudding.

Then he heard the gentle crinkle of a newspaper in the end stall at the higher end of the slanted floor that seemed unaffected by the flood.

"What's been going on in here?" he demanded of the anonymous stall dweller.

The newspaper gently crinkled again and a voice floated through the air.

"Well," came the quiet answer, "it seems that a flush beat a full house."

Men

~~~~~~~~~~~

While women's humor appears to be more refined than men's, a man's humor simply heads in the opposite direction because it plays to a different tune—usually involving bodily wind instruments. Manly humor binds men together in a secret brotherhood. What the fairer sex may view as raunchy, revolting, or crude, men consider to be eloquent, whimsical, and even delightfully musical. Famous composers of the Baroque period experimented and tested tunes emanating from one end as the other end conceived these melodies. Conception and execution were virtually simultaneous.

During the Ice Age, the discovery of bodily noises and the haunting echoes that reverberated inside the caves left an indelible impact as early men did their best to out-do each other; the louder the echo achieved, the greater the applause. Male team spirit in the lower forty-eight, buoyed by man's competitive nature and a solid appreciation of acoustics, may have led to the eventual establishment of what we now hail as *"the Boston Pops."*

In caveman days, before whistling was discovered, bodily noises were a good way to keep track of family members' whereabouts. Common bodily sounds could be heard through the underbrush, drifting off mountain tops, and

159

echoing through canyons. A mom with many kids could distinguish between them by their tonal releases.

Wild man honed all his five senses and relied upon them in a hostile 'kill or be killed' environment. He used them to obtain food and as a means to protect his family from the ravages of mammoths, saber-toothed tigers, bears, and a bad neighborhood. It is surmised that Nature selected the more musically inclined for survival, as emanations could be used both for warning sounds as well as for defense.

Taken out of context, gaseous digestive releases, commonly known as farts, did not bode well with the elders and leaders of tribes. Barks, blasts, or booms were not acceptable as a proper exchange of social pleasantries, and rarer still were they permitted as small talk. In fact some detonations were considered insulting or even interpreted as an act of war. Indeed, archeologists have determined that bloodshed often developed before the offensive "blast" had expired, yea, was still ringing in the ear. Ironically, natural selection may actually have come down to what one had for lunch and whether or not war was waged as a result.

New love was often spurred on by 'inflatulation' and smiled at by adults. It was also common for Cro-Magnon parents to recognize their own offspring by the higher, more innocent flatulent notes they produced (along with popular tunes or jingles they composed during play and adopted as their own). Today scientists speculate this parenting talent could even foretell a childhood abnormality and nip it in the bud. They went on to suggest, had it not been for auditory bodily emanations, evolution may have passed us by.

Men

Before one walks, one must crawl. And likewise, before one talks, one must grunt. Before words, people relied on a vocabulary of grunts. Noticeable accents that embellished the grunt could often determine where an individual came from. Some grunts and grumbles added the "r" sound while other grunts omitted it. If one were innovative, he could grunt, as it were, from either end, both as an alternating synchronized duet, or as a bold solo with backup harmony. There were angry grunts, happy grunts, love grunts, the grunt of pain, grunts of joy, and of course the burp-grunt, when etiquette came into play.

A well-timed belch meant "all was well", but a report from the lower abdominal region (in one of the major keys) was the final word signifying the hors d'oeuvres were mouth-watering, the mammoth rump cooked to perfection, the wine exquisite, the company enchanting, and the conversation stimulating. The absence of a grunt however, relayed its own sinister implications.

For centuries, stories were passed down from days of old as families and clans gathered around the campfire at night, safe and protected. Hunting stories were pantomimes for the most part, while grunts, burps (and worse) were used as gestures that literally added style and flare to the evening performance.

The precursor of today's fireworks demonstrations, the narrator/performer might jump right through the fire while releasing a volatile volley of gas that would ignite like an afterburner on an F22. This stunning performance never failed to evoke enthusiastic "ooohs" and "ahhs" from the delighted audience and even had a positive effect on the local economy. The concession stands did a phenomenal business during the show and when they ran out of fire and ice, they would have to send out for more. A general sense of security and camaraderie prevailed.

Whether accidental or deliberate, the timing and musical rendition of the exiting gas determined the height of its success. The timid flatulent-flute was frowned upon while the self-important trumpet would wow the crowd, especially if men or children were present. And as sure as the sun would come up, the crowd would settle down and inevitably a rogue composer in the audience would upstage the entertainer with a well-timed trumpet blast that would abruptly ignite the assembly like a keg of gunpowder all over again. It's in our DNA.

Today, these powers still exist, imparting the same age-old lessons in events both large and small. The contagious element in a robust belly laugh spreads through crowds like wildfire.

Words are rarely spoken in men's rooms, yet some things say all that needs to be said. Once the anal trumpet sounds, it is not uncommon to hear a chorus of laughter erupt among strangers as control is lost and mayhem restored. This small ditty says it all.

Comedians can pour out their heart on stage
and perform most magnificent art.
But to hear an audience really roar,
a man has only to fart.

Men

Used properly, the fart can bring people together with tears of laughter and cries of exclamation. Used improperly..... well, we won't go there. Man is now considered a civilized being and the object of modern society was to put the "art" in fart.

On one such occasion, I experienced a bond with total strangers uniting as one beneath the cloak of choke, the umbrella of wind, the snag of gag. I was attending a wedding in an old hotel where many had tied the knot. This stately place was ancient and in some respects well-worn, but it still clung to a certain class. The wedding ceremony was to be held at one end of the building and the reception was a short walk down a wide Grand Hall onto a flower-bedecked mezzanine nearby.

Along this broad hallway I found a memorable men's room, perhaps the largest I've ever seen, including the ones at O'Hare International. It was so large, in fact, that it had an entrance and an exit to avoid collisions. There must have been twenty urinals lining the outside wall to the right and ten stalls directly opposite on the left. The next room was a maze of sinks and mirrors and hot air fans with nozzles that could be pointed in any direction except straight. It was a full house with every facility in use and small lines forming nearby.

Polite company has certain restrictions and I had decided before I even entered the room that I was going in with only one purpose: to fart... to fart and flee, as it were. There would be no reason to stick around and I knew my welcome would likely be revoked on the spot anyway, so the strategy here was to attack and retreat immediately before anyone realized what happened.

163

Bowlful of Laughs

The wedding was a black tie affair and going to the bathroom would be nearly as difficult as in a ski lodge where the customary "layers of clothing work best". An example was the cumbersome cummerbund, a useless accoutrement and yet one more thing to be dealt with, but I had no intentions of removing any of what I had so meticulously put on.

It's a wise man who can tell ahead of time exactly what the lower intestine has planned. Over-confident men are slapped right into place by their innards along the trail to manhood and instantly humbled as they assign a new respect for their nether regions, which are really what is in the driver's seat. Woe unto those who discover firsthand the dangers involved in considering the breakdown of the word "assume". But I was always a man's man. I was safe, I was wise, and my instincts paid off. I knew my intestinal tract like I knew the Schuylkill Expressway.

I have no idea what goes on in ladies' rooms, but I know libraries could learn a lesson from the deafening silence in a typical men's room. Once inside a stall, men rely on legs as well as arms. Toilet seats are raised with the instep of the shoe and with the dexterity of a neurosurgeon. Toilet handles are flushed in similar fashion. The less that one comes in contact with in such locations the better, but I was prepared. I planned a "touch and go" as test pilots call it. That means to bring the aircraft in fast and low as if for a landing but as soon as it touches down, then gun it and take back off again. This was my mission, except that when entering this men's room, what I found inside was anything but typical.

164

Men

Upon entering, I found myself in the Taj Mahal of bathrooms. It had a vaulted ceiling, immaculate tile walls, a spit-shined floor, bright modern light fixtures, and wafting on the breeze was a vague fragrance of something like lavender or sandalwood. I even detected a soft background score of classical music. Mozart, I think.

The room was a veritable beehive of activity, with a decidedly aristocratic clientele. At least thirty men from this black tie event were present, all formally attired in black and white and looking for all the world like a sea of giant penguins. This did not seem the proper place to do what I was about to do, but I was past the point of no return. The runway was in view. If I chickened out now I'd be risking an intestinal explosion.

With my escape planned, I came in through the grand entrance and took a few steps towards the exit door, but kept an eye on where I had just entered. Once the door closed completely I let loose with what some might refer to as "an ill wind that blows no good". My common man's staccato "BOOM BOOM TRA BOOM" was instantly met with an awkward silence – and for one long moment I feared for my life.

But the next moment, the entire world before me erupted in a deafening roar of laughter from this huge audience of complete strangers, and soon everyone began howling, with tears starting to run down their cheeks. I was sorry I had no encore.

I smiled humbly, threw out my chest, and strutted past the crowd through the exit and back into the Grand Hall.

As the door began closing behind me in slow motion, a spontaneous cheering applause from within broke out on the heels of my departure as I started down the hallway back to the reception—and rings in my ears to this day. What a great crowd!

-The End-

www.ingramcontent.com/pod-product-compliance
Lightning Source LLC
Chambersburg PA
CBHW052045090426

42739CB00010B/2050